Women, Feminism, and Islam

Adeel Zeerak

ISBN: 1492235504
ISBN 13: 9781492235507
Library of Congress Control Number: 2013921482
CreateSpace Independent Publishing Platform
North Charleston, South Carolina

Dedication

I cannot think of a better person to dedicate this book to than the individual under whose feet lies my heaven;[1] my mother **Raisa Khanam Nighat**.
You were, are and will remain the best school for me.

Acknowledgement

I am thankful to all those who helped or guided me in any manner in writing or publishing this book.

Notably, Mufti Nazeer Ahmed (Advocate), Chaudary Bilal Bin Iqbal, Mr. Aslam Soni, Abu Summaiyah, Ms. Asiyeh Kashany and Mr. Farrukh Hassan.

My father, Abdul Hafeez Qureshi (late), who played a great part in my upbringing and education.

My mother, Raisa Khanam Nighat, whose prayers, guidance and encouragement has given me the strength to pursue my endeavors.

My other family members, including my wife Dr. Zunairah Rais and my two wonderful kids Ahmed Zeerak Qureshi and Muhammad Zeerak Qureshi who are always a source of inspiration for me.

My sister Ambareena Urooj, my niece Ayesha Qureshi, and my brother's wife Subia Wahab Zuberi.

My colleague, Ms. Saira Ihsan Khwaja, for reviewing and editing of the entire book before publishing. Her candor in giving remarks would at times feel like a direct blow. But her constructive criticism is what was needed for removing unwanted elements and unnecessarily long winding sentences, ensuring that the flow in my book was maintained.

May Allah (s.w.t. [1]) reward all of them with His blessings and mercy in this world and the Hereafter.

Adeel Zeerak

Table of Contents

Foreword

With the name of Allah, the All-Merciful, the Very-Merciful.

Both men and women are the wonderful creation of the Almighty God. Both the genders play an important role in a society and are indispensable for its proper functioning. Both are therefore important and deserve respect, honor and good treatment from society. Unfortunately, throughout the history of mankind, women had to face much cruelty and injustice in this male dominated world.

There are many groups and individuals existing today who work for women's rights. One such group consists of the Western feminists. Their efforts are mostly secular and therefore most of them do not consider taking guidance from religions in resolving women issues. Not all their concepts and actions are in complete harmony as there are areas in which they have serious disagreements.

Although the modern Feminist movement has done a lot to bring awareness of women's rights to masses in the Western societies, some of their concepts are highly controversial and tend to go in wrong directions. The term 'Feminism' may be widely understood in the West but is not very much clear to the people living in other parts of the world. Some people think that feminism is a totally wrong phenomenon as they think it only promotes nudity, vulgarity, homosexuality, and the like amongst women. My reply to such people is that not everything coming from the West is wrong.

Islam propagates that it is a religion based on pure Divine Guidance therefore it has a potential to solve all worldwide problems. Muslims therefore assert that Islam is a religion that gives full rights to women and does not exploit them like is done in the West. However, on the other hand, many people in the West think that Islam oppresses women. Any individual whose source of Islamic knowledge has been the Western media, has a perception that Islamic teachings are misogynistic.

I had formally studied the Islamic point of view about women during my study of Islam from various Muslim scholars. My secular knowledge, however, regarding women started with my involvement in a UNDP project on 'Gender Based Governance Systems' in 2009. I was involved in a training project for Government of Pakistan officials on basic gender related concepts and gender sensitive project planning skills. In 2013 I was involved in preparing and delivering a training for women staff of an international NGO on the topic of 'Feminism and its linkages with social issues'. My knowledge on gender issues from a Western perspective greatly increased with my involvement in such projects. And with the passage of time, I became fully conversant on women issues from both secular and religious perspectives. Most authors tend to either have only the secular point of view or only the religious point of view on the topic.

After the successful publication of my first book 'Islam: A Superior System of Life', I was contemplating which topic to highlight in my next book. I finally decided to write a book on women as I felt that there are many misconceptions among the masses on this critical topic especially regarding the Islamic point of view that need to be addressed. I have attempted to tackle this extremely important topic from both the secular as well as the Islamic perspectives with the hope that this book will be highly informative for the readers.

Adeel Zeerak

Chapter 1
Women Are Women

Women hold up half the Sky
(Chinese proverb)

Some men openly admit their failure in understanding women. For example, Sigmund Freud (1856-1939), who is considered to be the founder of psychoanalysis, said, "The great question that has never been answered, and which I have not yet been able to answer despite my thirty years of research into the feminine soul, is: What does a woman want?" [1] According to CBS News, "British scientist Stephen Hawking has decoded some of the most puzzling mysteries of the universe but he has left one mystery for the rest of the world to solve: How he has managed to survive so long with such a crippling disease. As for Hawking himself, he says there is only one enduring mystery of the universe he has found impossible to crack: Women. At least, that is what he told New Scientist magazine in an interview for his upcoming 70th birthday celebration when they asked what he thinks about the most during the day." [2]

In January of 2013, I was in Islamabad (capital of Pakistan) for conducting a two days training on the topic of Feminism for an international anti-poverty non-governmental organization [3], whose primary objective is to fight poverty worldwide. During the tea break of the training, one girl made a remark in front of me. She said, 'Women are just Women.' The statement of the girl was her spontaneous reaction after looking at the behavior of some women during the training and especially at that tea break, when she made this remark. The statement however was followed by another request of hers, "Please do not quote my words to the other ladies ..." as, she felt, some of them might be offended by this statement. Despite whatever some feminists might think, this statement of hers regarding women should not be considered as an insult for women. There is nothing wrong with women if they are different from men. In fact this is part of their feminine beauty. And similarly being masculine and different from women is part of their beauty for the men. Both the genders are important and wonderful creations of the Almighty God with a purpose behind their creation that defines the respective role they play in society.

Tamara McClintock Greenberg, Psy.D., M.S., is a clinical psychologist in San Francisco. In her article 'Differences between men and women: *Talking about Inequalities in the Shadow of the Feminist Movement*' writes:

"As a woman and a psychologist who has treated women and couples in the last two decades, I find that as I get older, I make a lot more comments to both male and female patients about how the sexes differ. …Yet, I find myself sometimes experiencing a curious anxiety when I point out sex and gender differences between women and men. The way men and women listen and talk is just one example. I can get even more anxious when I imply that men process emotions differently and they respond to feelings in a way that can seem foreign to us women. … This begs the question, are women the same as men? Are we different? And if so, can we live with the idea of difference in a post 1970's feminist world?"

She further explains, "Just because men and women have different ways of thinking about things does not make women inferior. It would be nice if men and women can both acknowledge the ways we are unique and take a stance that is more understanding. We all have different strengths." [4]

I remember during my childhood days, my cousin's daughter while playing with us started to tease one of my male cousins by saying 'Girl girl, you are a girl'. She wanted to degrade him by calling him a girl. I immediately asked, "Is there anything wrong about being a girl? Do you think girls are inferior?" She could not give any reply. There is nothing wrong in being a female. Women who try to copy men in various areas of life are perhaps suffering from some sort inferiority complex. As I said that both (males and females) are the wonderful creatures of Allah s.w.t, the Almighty God. And the Creator has guided both of them regarding their appropriate behavior in a society. And this guidance is present today with all of us in the form of Islam.

Nearly 50% of the world's population consists of females. Although men and women both are suffering but if we compare the two sexes, we find women comparatively in worse condition. Generally speaking, women throughout the world are suffering from various forms of exploitation, cruelty and injustice. Making efforts for women rights is therefore very much required. No segment of a society including that of women should suffer. This is our duty as human beings.

Women are all around us (men) as our mothers, sisters, daughters, and wives. They are playing wonderful roles in our lives and we therefore should be grateful to them. We cannot gain true happiness in life when we are surrounded by unhappy individuals. We have to share happiness with the people around us for the sake of our own happiness and self-satisfaction. If the women around us, like our wives, are not happy then how can they make us and our family happy?

In our part of the world it is said that a mother is the first madressah (school) for a child. These statements are cent percent right. If we want our children to get the right training and education from the very beginning, in order to make them effective members of the society, we need to have good mothers to raise them. Our personality is mostly developed in our childhood days, most of which is spent with our mothers. Even in later part of our lives, mothers play an important role in our development. Perhaps this is the reason why the celebrated French emperor and general Napoleon Bonaparte said, "Let France have good mothers, and she will have good sons."

Many readers of this book might be Muslim men whether they are practicing Islam in its true spirit or not. I also want to remind these men through this book that for them it is their religious duty to take care of women. We need to respect women and to take care of them if we really want to practice Islam. Islam is not only about some beliefs, worships, and rituals. Islam is a comprehensive system of life which also consists of dealings and showing good behaviour with the people around us. And who is more close to a husband than a wife and other immediate family members. The Prophet Muhammad (PBUH [5]) said, "The worst of the people is he who makes life hard for his family members." (Kanz-ul-Aamal)

Despite all these good reasons to take care of women, we witness quite a grim picture all over the world. Generally speaking women throughout the world are suffering. In this modern world of space exploration and the internet, they are still in bad shape with respect to poverty, education, and health care. Violence against women is also a big problem both in developed and underdeveloped countries. Many women are being battered, raped, sexually abused, kidnapped, trafficked, or murdered. Many people are making efforts for women rights throughout the world. Some of their efforts are in the right direction; however there are areas where their efforts are going astray and are thus unintentionally further deteriorating the condition of women.

Being a management trainer and consultant, I have conducted numerous trainings on various topics including the topic of 'Gender'. However the topic of 'Feminism' was quite new to me when I was asked to deliver a two days session on Feminism and other related social issues. The audience was Pakistan-based, female staff from the local chapter of the international anti-poverty non-governmental organization. I conducted a lot of research for preparing for the topic. I collected data from various local and foreign sources regarding women. Despite my preparation, I was nervous. There were many objectives in my mind that needed to be covered during the training. Some of them were:

- To inform the participants about the basics of modern Feminism and feminist movements throughout the world.
- To clarify that we need to understand 'Western Feminism' carefully to filter out some negative aspects that are also coming under the umbrella of Feminism. Not everything is wrong but some of the modern feminist concepts are serving the purpose of further degrading women and exploiting them. Even many modern feminists are against such concepts, which include equating men

to women in every aspect of life or becoming lesbians or being part of the pornographic culture or becoming prostitutes in the name of 'Women Liberation'. As is the case with various concepts originating from the West, modern Feminism is also a mix of rights and wrongs. One must differentiate between the two and reject what is wrong and accept what is right. If there are efforts by feminists groups for stopping violence against women or for ending sexual exploitation of women, then I think all such efforts of theirs are highly commendable.

- One important objective was to inform the participants about what Islam says about women. I also wanted to clarify many Islamic concepts that are wrongly portrayed by the enemies of Islam to build an impression that Islam is partly or wholly against women. We also need to differentiate between Islam and Muslims. It is not necessary that all the current practices in Muslim majority areas are part of Islamic teachings. In fact many practices are personal interpretations and mutilations by individuals or groups that are against the teachings of Islam. Islam is not against women, no argument about it. If that were the case then the majority of the people in USA and Europe who are converting to Islam would not consist of women.

The post-training feedback of the participants showed their receptiveness to the ideas introduced to them during the training. I was content for having successfully achieved my training objectives. These same objectives were also in my mind among others while writing this book 'Women, Feminism, and Islam'.

Chapter 2

Problems Faced By Women

"As for the women, though we scorn & flout em,
we may live with, but cannot live without 'em".
(Frederic Reynolds, *British dramatist)*

CONDITION OF WOMEN

As a community, women throughout the world are suffering. Although men are also victim of the exploitive societal systems, but as compared to women they are in a better position. Following UNDP data supports this fact:

- Of the world's 1 billion poorest people, three-fifths are women and girls.
- Of the 960 million adults in the world who cannot read, two-thirds are women.
- Half a million women die and at least 9 million more suffer serious injuries or disabilities from preventable complications of pregnancy and childbirth.
- Women everywhere typically earn less than men. They are concentrated in low-paying jobs and earn less for the same work. [1]

The quoted data portrays a gloomy picture throughout the world on the condition of women with respect to poverty, education, and health. Violence against women is another area which causes suffering and trauma for women and therefore requires some discussion here.

VIOLENCE AGAINST WOMEN

The United Nations defines the term 'violence against women' as any act of gender-based violence that results in, or is likely to result in, physical, sexual or psychological harm or suffering to women, including threats of such acts, coercion or arbitrary deprivation of liberty, whether occurring in public or in private life. [2] According to a newspaper report, globally one out of every three women experiences violence in her lifetime. [3] Books, news, documentaries and movies by some Westerners on this topic give an impression that violence against women is only a problem of the underdeveloped world. On the contrary violence against women is a worldwide problem and this is evident from the following figures of a developed nation by a US based feminist organization:

"Violence against women is a worldwide yet still hidden problem. Freedom from the threat of harassment, battering, and sexual assault is a concept that most of us have a hard time imagining because violence is such a deep part of our cultures and our lives. Consider these facts:

- Battering is the leading cause of injury to women aged 15 - 44 in the U.S.
- The FBI, which gathers data from law enforcement officials, indicated that 102,555 women were victims of rape in 1990.
- In contrast to the FBI data, the Rape in America study estimates that 683,000 women are raped every year.
- Approximately 50% of the homeless women and children in this country are on the streets because of violence in their homes.
- One-fifth to one-half of U.S. women were sexually abused as children at least once, most of them by an older male relative.
- Nearly two-thirds of women who receive public assistance ("welfare") have been abused by an intimate partner at some time in their adult lives." [4]

Similarly violence against women is also a problem of underdeveloped countries, for example, well-known Indian activist Kamla Bhasin informs, "In India girls are being killed in the womb, in millions. About 35 million are missing. Rape cases are seen to be on the rise. We feel violence against women is the biggest civil war in the world, where a billion people are violated in one way or another." [5]

Violence against women could be perpetrated by assailants of either genders, family members, or even the State itself. Whether right or wrong, I have heard many people including women making the statement; "It is a woman who is the enemy of a woman". One girl however added a qualifier to this statement. According to her this statement is partially applicable in cities where husbands are more educated and caring towards women. But other women like mothers-in-law, daughters-in-law, and sisters-in-law are also the cause of the problem. She said that in the rural areas, men generally show cruelty towards all the women around them. I cannot say with surety as to what is the percentage of truth behind such observation of hers, but I can say with surety that a man is not responsible for violence against women in every case.

Forms of violence:

Violence against women can take various forms. Some of its manifestations are:

- Domestic violence
- Torture
- Harassment
- Sexual assault/Rape
- Incest and sexual abuse of children
- Abduction / kidnapping
- Trafficking
- Murder
- Threat to life
- Acid throwing
- Burning alive
- Illegal custody

The following text discusses some of these types of violence with facts and figures to have a better understanding of the issue.

Domestic violence:- I am reproducing below some paragraphs by a feminist group to give you an idea about the prevalence of domestic violence in the world:

"Battering, often referred to as domestic violence, is one of the most common and least reported crimes in the world. Battering happens to women of every age, race, class, and nationality. It is done by the men we marry or date who beat us; by our sons and nephews who bully us and slap us around; and by male relatives who verbally harass and degrade us.

Battering takes many forms and includes a range of threatening and harmful behavior. It may take the form of verbal and emotional abuse, with the direct or implied threat of violence. Battering may include control of finances and one's physical freedom. It includes the destruction of objects and harm to pets. Battering may involve severe and frequent beatings or may happen occasionally. It may include slapping, punching, choking, kicking, or hitting with objects. Stalking can be a part of battering, especially if the woman has left the relationship. Battering may escalate to sexual assault and can ultimately end in murder. Battering can happen in new relationships at the dating stage and may continue into our elder years. As time passes, battering tends to increase in frequency and severity." [6]

Following are some of the statements by victims as mentioned in the same source;

"I have had glasses thrown at me. I have been kicked in the abdomen, kicked off the bed, and hit while lying on the floor—while I was pregnant. I have been whipped, kicked and thrown, picked up and thrown down again."

"I have been threatened when he's had a bad day—when he's had a good day."

"My very upper-middle-class, WASP father hit my mother drunkenly on an occasional Saturday night. Sunday morning she would explain away her bruises. I lived my whole childhood under this shadow--the possibility of violence, the sounds in the night, and the toll it took on me that she put up with it."

Incest and sexual abuse of children:- According to the same Feminist source:

"One common form of sexual abuse of children is incest, which has been defined as sexual contact that occurs between family members. Most incest occurs between older male relatives and younger female children in families of every class and color. Other instances of sexual abuse of children are most often committed by friends who have access to children within the family setting and by people normally trusted by parents: doctors, dentists, teachers, and babysitters. Incest and sexual abuse of children take many forms and may include sexually suggestive language; prolonged kissing, looking, and petting; vaginal and/or anal intercourse; and oral sex. Because sexual contact is often achieved without overt physical force, there may be no obvious signs of physical harm. A sexually abusive relationship is one over which a child or young woman has no control. A trusted family member or friend uses his power, as well as a child's love and dependence, to initiate sexual contact and often to ensure that the relationship continues and remains secret.

The extent of incest and childhood sexual abuse is difficult to measure because of lack of reporting and lack of memory. One study in which adults were asked to report on past incidents found that one in four girls and one in ten boys experienced sexual abuse. It is often very difficult to talk about incest or childhood sexual abuse. Some of us may never have told anyone, though the abuse may have continued for years. We may have dreaded family gatherings, where a particular uncle or family friend would come after us. For some of us, exploring our bodies with an older brother turned into a sexual encounter, after which we found ourselves feeling we had been taken advantage of. Sometimes a father, uncle, or teacher abused our sisters, and we didn't find out for years. Every survivor has her own story, and every story is valid." [7]

Following are some statements of the victims from the same feminist source:

"It's been really hard to figure out how this has affected me with men. I've had a hard time figuring out who is safe and who isn't. Now the only way I will sleep with someone is if I can have complete control. I need permission to feel uncomfortable with certain sexual acts."

"I often feel hopeless and suicidal. My father treated me with such violence that this is the only way I know to treat myself. I'm learning better ways now, but it's difficult."

"My barter with my brother was that he could do sex on me to practice for his girlfriends. I consented not because I enjoyed it but because I was afraid to be alone when my parents went out....I never even thought of talking about it. That just couldn't be done."

Trafficking:- The United Nations defines trafficking as the recruitment, transportation, transfer, harboring, or receipt of persons, by means of the threat or use of force or other forms of coercion, of abduction, of fraud, of deception, of the abuse of power or of a position of vulnerability or of the giving or receiving of payments or benefits to achieve the consent of a person having control over another person, for the purpose of exploitation. Exploitation shall include, at a minimum, the exploitation of the prostitution of others or other forms of sexual exploitation, forced labor or services, slavery or practices similar to slavery, servitude or the removal of organs. [8]

According to the US department of State, an estimated 600,000 to 800,000 men, women, and children are trafficked across international borders each year. Among them approximately 80 percent are women and girls and up to 50 percent are minors. The data also illustrate that the majority of transnational victims are trafficked into commercial sexual exploitation. With a focus on transnational trafficking in persons, however, these data fail to include millions of victims around the world who are trafficked within their own national borders. [9]

Catherine A. Mackinnon is an American feminist, scholar, lawyer, teacher and activist. While mentioning global women trafficking problem, she writes, "Are women human yet? If women were human, would we be a cash crop shipped from Thailand in containers into New York's brothel...? ...When will women be human?" [10]

Sexual assault/rape:- Sexual assault is any form of sexual activity committed against a woman's will. A rapist can use force or threats of force for the purpose. The cases of rape/sexual assault mostly go unreported. The common reasons given for not reporting these crimes are the belief that it is a private or personal matter and the fear of reprisal from the assailant. Following are some of the comments of the female victims of rape as mentioned by the feminist organization:

"I feel like a part of me died, like my life will never be the same. Because I was raped by my boyfriend as a teen, I feel like I missed the chance to have a normal adolescence when everyone says those should have been the best years of my life."

"I barely manage to function all day. When I wake up in the morning I just want to stay in bed. I feel like there is a dark cloud following me around. I feel sad and can't remember what it feels like to be happy."

"My life is not my own anymore; what's the use of making decisions when I have no power to change my life?"

"I close my eyes to go to sleep and all I can see is the rape. I feel as though it is happening to me over and over."

"Like many victims of sexual attacks, I was silenced by my shame, guilt, & the mistaken belief, reinforced by the police and society in general ... that I was 'responsible' for what these men did to me. It is that silence that revictimizes rape & incest victims, over & over again, & I won't be silent anymore." [11]

PROBLEMS FACED BY
WORKING WOMEN

Women who choose to work outside their homes have another set of problems to deal with. The problems faced by them are at the actual workplace, at home, and in between the two places. Some of the problems that working women face are:

Discrimination:

One of problems faced by working women throughout the world is the problem of sexual discrimination. Women throughout the world are concentrated to lower level jobs. Very few women are holding the managerial and decision-making positions in organizations. Following are two examples of this problem:

In the United States women earn on average 71% as much as men do. This gap exists in part because women have traditionally found work in lower-paying occupations such as teaching, retailing, and nursing. Part of the difference in earnings results from women leaving the workforce to have and care for children or parents, and part probably results from discrimination. [12]

Patrice C. McMahon is a writer and a political science professor at the University of Nebraska-Lincoln. He mentions in his book regarding Russian women of the Soviet Union, "By the late 1980s, almost 80 percent of women in the Soviet Union were active participants in the workforce, a figure higher than any other country in Western Europe or North America, except Sweden. Nontheless, despite its loyalty to equal rights and its ability to increase the number of women in higher education and in scientific and technical fields, Soviet women were not any more successful than women in the West in reaching positions of power. (Rendel 1981; Janova 1992) ... In the 1970s approximately 4 percent of

working women in the United States workforce were managers, officials or proprietors; and in the United Kingdom female managers never
exceeded 1 percent of all managers in the country. Yet in Soviet Union,
as throughout the Socialist bloc, women were less successful in achieving
leading positions in the economy. While representing over 50 percent of
the workforce, only 0.5 percent of managers or directors were women
(Wlochik 1981)."

Patrice C. McMahon further explains, "Soviet women not only worked
extensively in the home, which undoubtedly hampered their upward
mobility in the paid sector, but they also experienced overt and subtle
forms of discrimination by their colleagues and superiors. Throughout
the society, but especially with the Communist Party there was a reluctance to put women in positions of authority... In all sectors of the
economy, women in the Soviet Union experienced the 'glass ceiling'
syndrome and were under-represented in positions of power relative to
their share of the workforce. The inability of women to become high-
level decision-makers was clearly not due to inferior education. In fact,
among individuals in the workforce, women were more educated than
men." [13]

Sexual harassment:

Another problem faced by working women is the problem of sexual
harassment. In a survey of 607 women by the National Association for
Female Executives, 60% reported having experienced sexual harassment. According to the director general of the International Labor
Organization (ILO) based in Geneva, Switzerland, "Research findings
in 23 industrialized countries around the globe demonstrated that sexual
harassment is a pervasive problem affecting a considerable proportion
of working women."' [14]

Some facts and figures regarding this problem as mentioned by the feminist organization are:

"Sexual harassment is any unwanted sexual attention a woman experiences. It includes leering, pinching, patting, repeated comments, subtle suggestions of a sexual nature, and pressure for dates. Sexual harassment can occur in any situation where men have power over women: welfare workers with clients, doctors with patients, police officers with women members of a police force, or teachers with students. In the workplace, the harasser may be an employer, a supervisor, a co-worker, a client, or a customer. Sexual harassment can escalate; women who are being sexually harassed are at risk of being physically abused or raped. Consider these facts:

According to the U.S. Department of Labor, some 50 to 80% of women in the U.S. experience some form of sexual harassment during their academic or work lives. Some examples are:

In a survey of girls in middle schools and high schools that was distributed in Seventeen, 83% of the girls who responded reported instances of sexual harassment in school.

Sexual harassment is a powerful way for men to undermine and control us. Attitudes of race and class superiority can result in a feeling by white men that they are entitled to sexually harass women of color or employees from a "lower" class or different background. There is an implicit (and sometimes explicit) message that our refusal to comply with the harasser's demands will lead to work-related reprisals. These can include escalation of harassment; poor work assignments; sabotaging of projects; denial of raises, benefits, or promotion; and sometimes the loss of the job with only a poor reference to show for it. Harassment can drive women out of a particular job or out of the workplace altogether.

Socializing at work too often includes flirting or joking about sex. Although it may be a pleasant relief from routine or a way to communicate with someone we are interested in, this banter can become insulting or demeaning. It becomes sexual harassment when it creates a hostile, intimidating, or pressured working environment.

There is such a taboo in many workplaces and schools against identifying sexual harassment for what it is that many of us who experience it are at first aware only of feeling stressed. We may experience headaches, anxieties, or resistance to going to work in the morning. It may take us a while to realize that these symptoms come from our being sexually harassed. We often respond by feeling isolated and powerless, afraid to say no or to speak out because we fear either that we somehow are responsible or that we won't receive help in facing possible retaliation. But when we take the risk and talk with other women, we often find that they are being harassed, too (or have been), and have similar responses to ours.

Joan is a 43-year-old black woman who works as a waitress in a bar and restaurant. She often feels isolated, as many of her co-workers are white and have racist attitudes. A customer who comes in every day begins to flirt with Joan, making suggestive comments about her clothing and physical appearance. Unnerved by his comments, she tries not to show it because she doesn't want to lose any tip money. Often he grabs at her and touches her when she walks by. She feels so anxious at work that her stomach hurts, and she starts to call in sick more and more. She knows she needs to figure something out or she'll eventually lose her job.

One 16-year-old girl described her experience: It came to the point where I was skipping almost all of my classes, therefore getting me kicked out of the honors program. I dreaded school each morning, I started to wear clothes that wouldn't flatter my figure, and I kept to myself. I'd cry every night when I got home, and I thought I was a loser....Sometimes the teachers were right there when it was going on. They did nothing....I felt very angry that these arrogant, narrow-minded people never took the time to see who really was inside." [15]

Increased responsibilities:

Working women generally have to cope up with dual responsibilities. They have responsibilities at home and at the job that they are doing outside their homes.

Dr. Henry Makow, a Jewish writer in Canada and the inventor of the board-game Scruples, in his article 'Debauchery of American Womenhood' criticizes, "Feminism teaches woman that feminine nature has resulted in 'oppression' and that she should convert to male behavior instead. The result: a confused and aggressive woman with a large chip on her shoulder, unfit to become a wife or mother." [16]

Dr. Makow is very critical to modern feminist movement. He points out various problems attached to feminism which would be analyzed in the later chapters of this book. However in his quoted statement where he has said "…with a large chip on her shoulder" seems to be well supported by data.

Similarly Patrice C. McMahon explains the experience of Russian working women with facts and figures: "Thus the implicit meaning of women's liberation came to mean increased responsibilities on all fronts rather than deliverance from traditional toils. … In 1990 the average Russian woman spend approximately 35 hours per week on housework and childcare and 38 hours in paid employment; throughout the week, women spent nearly 48 hours more than men on housework and childcare each week (Fong 1993:19). In rural areas, where homes often lack modern conveniences, such as sewer systems or electricity, women are believed to work approximately 8 hours per day on domestic chores in addition to 7 hours at the state farm compared with men who work 2 hours at home and 7 ½ hours outside the home (Mirovitskaya 1993b: 27-30)." [17]

The US data reveals the same phenomenon. Debora Spar, who was a faculty member at Harvard Business School for nearly 20 years, writes in her article, "Another piece of the puzzle sits closer to home, where parity remains frustratingly elusive and women still consistently log more hours than their mates. Between 1965 and 2000, the number of working mothers in the United States rose from 45 to 78 percent of all mothers, and the average time that an American woman spent in the paid labor force increased from 9 to 25 hours a week. Yet women were still devoting nearly 40 hours a week to family care: housework, child care, shopping.

Men, by contrast, spent only 21, most of which were devoted to fairly discrete and flexible tasks like mowing the lawn, washing the car, and tossing softballs with the kids." [18]

Neglected children:

It is difficult for a woman to work outside her home especially if she has small children and she does not want to have any sort of compromise in their upbringing. In many cases compromises are made by women that result in another type of social problem. The children do not develop a typical relationship that should have been there between a child and a mother. A better relationship is built with the television with which they spend most of their time. I have seen many cases where such children became rebellious with their parents, especially mothers, who did not have time for them. Such parents had money to buy expensive toys but what was lacking was the time for their children.

Our local television channel was once showing a mother complaining about her son who used to batter her. She had to run for safer places to prevent herself from the battering of her only son. Some discussion with the mother revealed that she was a divorcee, doing three jobs at a time to earn a lot of money for herself and her son, during his childhood days. She was complaining that she gave everything like expensive toys, books, etc, to her son. The only thing that seemed to be lacking was that she had no time for him.

Greedy family members:

Some women do not want to work but their greedy husbands or in-laws and other family members force them to work for the sake of money. In our part of the world this problem is very pervasive in the financially lower classes. Women are generally employed at other homes as maids. Their husbands are either not employed anywhere or not employed consistently. Instead of being grateful to their hardworking wives, they usually mistreat them. Occasional battering of wives is a common phenomenon in such families. In some rural areas nearly all the work is done by women. This includes working on the agricultural lands, doing all the house work, and raising children. Their husbands do nothing but spend most of their time in local restaurants, watching television and smoking, and in some cases consuming drugs.

Sometimes greedy husbands even have control over the cheque books of the wife's salary accounts. Thus even the money earned by the wife is not under her control.

Problems on the way:

Women also face various problems on her way to the workplace and back to home. These problems range from being stared to being sexually assaulted. This is also a global problem.

According to a feminist source: "Several myths can prevent us from defending ourselves effectively against a physical assault. They include the myth that the assailant is invulnerable, that greater physical strength will decide who will prevail, that we don't know how to defend ourselves. Yet, as women we have defended ourselves against attack in many instances. One woman frightened off three adolescent males who were following her along a city street by turning quickly and letting out a bloodcurdling yell. Another stopped a would-be assailant with a kick to the midsection. A young girl sitting on the train found a wayward hand on her knee. She took the man's wrist in her grasp, raised his hand high in the air, and said loudly enough for the entire car to hear, 'Who does this belong to?' He got off at the next stop. ...Countless daily acts of violence create a climate of fear and powerlessness that limits women's freedom of action and controls many of the movements of our lives. The threat of male violence continues to keep us from stepping out from behind the traditional roles that we, as women, have been taught. Violence and the threat of violence keep us 'in our place.'" [19]

MALE VIOLENCE TOWARDS WOMEN

According to the feminist organization, "One man's violence against one woman may seem to result from his individual psychological problems, sexual frustration, unbearable life pressures, or some innate urge toward aggression. Though each of these 'reasons' has been used to explain and even justify male violence, they oversimplify a complex reality: men have been taught to relate to the world in terms of dominance and control, and they have been taught that violence is an acceptable method of maintaining control, resolving conflicts, and expressing anger. When a boss sexually harasses an employee, he exerts his power to restrict her freedom to work and improve her position. When a battering husband uses beatings to confine his wife to the home and to prevent her from seeing friends and family or from pursuing outside work, he exerts dominance and control. When men rape women, they act out of a wish to dominate or punish. Whether or not an individual man who commits an act of violence views it as an expression of power is not the point. The fact that so many individual men feel entitled to express their frustration or anger by being violent to so many individual women shows how deeply these lessons of dominance and violence have been learned." [20]

In many under-developed countries, tribal and feudal traditions provide support to customary practices, such as killing of women in the name of 'honor'. In these countries bad laws and governance allow perpetrators to often escape punishment. Vast numbers of cases are not registered by the police. The media only gets to hear about the most gruesome and shocking incidents.

Another problem is that violence against women is still considered as a 'private' matter. Women hesitate to speak out against the humiliation they suffer, or are afraid of more violence and hence demonstrate reluctance due to the risk of being embroiled in court proceedings for years on end.

LAWS TO PROTECT WOMEN

Many countries have laws to protect women. However, the problem is, in most countries although the laws are there, the mechanism to enforce them is deficient. Laws can only be successful if they are fully enforced by prosecutors, police, judges, health care and education experts. Laws and bills cannot work in a society that turns a blind eye to the plight of its women. Only when collaborative effort is made by law enforcers, judiciary and the civil society to bring about meaningful change, can women hope to attain the justice and dignity they have fought for.

There are still numerous cases of violence against women in developed countries despite good law enforcement mechanisms. Many crimes go unreported due to various reasons. This is because a country cannot deploy a police man in each and every place like individual homes to prevent cruelty against women. If we really want to protect women from violence, exploitation, and injustice, we must do more than just making laws and deploying enforcement mechanisms. We need to build awareness and educate everyone in an effort to solve this issue. We must try to change the mindset of the whole society. This would require character building efforts especially those of males, beginning from their early childhood.

We need to have God conscious people to prevent them from committing violence against women. Perhaps this is the reason why the short religious speech usually given during the Muslim wedding ceremony starts with the statement from Quran mentioning the term 'Taqwa' i.e fear of God. Only the God fearing people know that even if nobody is watching them at their homes, God is there to witness their good and bad deeds. And they will be ultimately accountable in front of God for all their actions in this world.

Therefore, we not only need to make legislation and design good enforcing mechanisms to prevent violence against women, but we also need to take some preventive measures in the form of awareness building, counselling and developing God councious people in the true spirit. Only then we can hope to develop a society free from any kind of violence against women.

Chapter 3

What is Feminism?

"I myself have never been able to find out precisely what femi-
nism is; I only know that people call me feminist whenever I
express sentiments that differentiate me from a doormat"

(Rebecca West, *English writer)* [1]

Feminism, in its various forms and concepts is a complex topic to understand. To give readers an idea about feminism, in this chapter I will give an overview of the topic without going into too much detail. I do not agree or disagree with all the feminist concepts discussed in this chapter but I have avoided giving my opinions during the various discussions on the topic. Some of the points later will be discussed in much detail in the subsequent chapters of this book alongside my views.

FEMINISM DEFINED

Defining feminism can be difficult, but a broad understanding of it includes the acting, speaking, writing, and advocating on behalf of women's rights and issues, and identifying injustice to women in the society. Feminist activists struggle for women's rights such as in contract law, property, and voting. They also promote bodily integrity, autonomy, and reproductive rights for women.

Like many other terms and concepts, various people define feminism in a slightly different ways; however, the underlying concept remains more or less the same. According to Oxford dictionary, "Feminism is a movement or theory that supports the rights of women." "Feminist is a noun and adjective of Feminism."

According to Wikipedia, "Feminism is a collection of movements & ideologies aimed at defining, establishing, and defending equal political, economic, and social rights for women. In addition, feminism seeks to establish equal opportunities for women in education and employment". "A feminist is an advocate or supporter of the rights and equality of women".

According to one feminist, feminism is, "A concern with women issues, awareness that women suffer discrimination at work, in the home and in society, and actions aimed at improving their lives".

While discussing about feminism we should keep in mind that modern day feminists are not the only one who talked about women's rights and issues. Throughout the history there were people and groups who did so. The people and activists who discussed or advanced women's issues prior to the existence of the modern feminist movement are sometimes labelled by some modern day feminists as 'proto-feminist'. Some, however, criticize the use of this term 'proto-feminist'. They argue that this term diminishes the importance of earlier contributions for women rights by people throughout the history. Some argue that feminism does not have a single, linear history as implied by terms such as 'proto-feminist' or 'post-feminist'.

Although all feminists claim to support women rights, not all of them have the same thinking process and concepts. There is a great variety among the feminists. There are radical feminists with extreme views regarding various issues and there are comparatively moderate ones. There are also some issues where feminists are very much divided, for example 'sexuality'. Their disagreement and controversy over this issue has even been given a term of 'feminist sex-wars', which would be discussed later in this chapter.

HISTORY OF FEMINISM [2]

The history of feminism involves the narrative of feminist movements and thinkers. The terms 'feminism' or 'feminist' first appeared in France and Netherlands in 1872. It appeared in the Great Britain in the 1890s, and in the United States in 1910. The Oxford English Dictionary mentions 1894 for the first appearance of the term "feminist" and 1895 for the term 'feminism'. The UK Daily News introduced the term 'feminist' to the English language, importing it from France and branding it as dangerous. Before that time, 'Woman's Rights' was probably the term most commonly used.

History of the modern Western feminist movements is usually divided into three eras known as 'three waves' of feminism. Each is described as dealing with different aspects of the same issues related to feminism. The first wave refers to the movement of the 19th through early 20th centuries, that dealt mainly with suffrage (right to vote), working conditions and educational rights for girls / women. The second wave of feminism (1960s-1980s) dealt with the inequality of laws, as well as cultural inequalities and the role of women in a society. The third wave (late 1980s - early 2000s), is seen as both a continuation of the second wave and a response to the perceived failures.

The first-wave focused primarily on gaining the right of women's suffrage, the right to be educated, better working conditions and also talked about double sexual standards. The term 'first-wave', was coined after the term 'second-wave feminism' began to be used to describe a newer feminist movement that focused as much on fighting social and cultural inequalities as further political inequalities.

Second-wave feminism refers to a period of feminist activity starting in the early 1960s that carried through the late 1980s. Second-Wave Feminism has existed continuously since then, and continues to coexist with the Third-Wave. Second-Wave saw cultural and political inequalities as inextricably linked. The movement encouraged women to understand aspects of their personal lives as deeply politicized, and reflective of a sexist structure of power. (Sexism is prejudice or discrimination based on a person's sex, behavior, conditions, or attitudes that foster stereotypes of social roles based on sex.) If first-wavers focused on absolute rights such as suffrage, second-wavers were largely concerned with other issues of equality, such as the end to sexual discrimination.

Third-wave began in the early 1990s. The movement arose as a response to what young women thought of as perceived failures of the second-wave feminism. Third-wave was also a response to the backlash against initiatives and movements created by the second-wave. Third-wave feminism seeks to challenge or avoid what it deems the second wave's 'essentialist' definitions of femininity, which according to them over-emphasized the experiences of upper middle class white women. (In philosophy, essentialism is the view that, for any specific entity such as a group of people, there is a set of incidental attributes all of which are necessary to its identity and function. The essentialist view on gender, sexuality, race, ethnicity, or other group characteristics is that they are fixed traits, discounting variation among group members as secondary.)

A post-structuralist interpretation of gender and sexuality is central to much of the ideology of the third wave. (Post-structuralism emerged in France during the 1960s as a movement critiquing structuralism. Structuralism is a theoretical paradigm emphasizing that elements of culture must be understood in terms of their relationship to a larger, overarching system or structure.) Third wavers often focus on 'micropolitics', and challenged the second wave's paradigm as to what is, or is not, good for females. (Micropolitics is the use of formal and informal power by individuals and groups to achieve their goals within organizations, as opposed to macropolitics.)

FEMINIST THEORY, MOVEMENTS, AND IDEOLOGIES

Feminist theory:

Feminist theory is the term used in relation to the Feminist movement. It is the extension of feminism into theoretical and philosophical areas. It comprises of works in a variety of disciplines, including anthropology, sociology, women studies, economics, literary criticism, art, history, psychoanalysis, and philosophy. The theory aims to understand gender inequality and focuses on gender politics, power relations, and sexuality. While providing a critique of the social and political relations in a society, a great deal of feminist theory also focuses on the promotion of women's rights and interests. Some of the themes explored in feminist theory include discrimination, stereotyping, objectification (especially sexual objectification), oppression, and patriarchy. Some of these concepts will be discussed later in this book.

Political movements:

Liberal feminism seeks individualistic equality of men and women through political and legal reform without altering the society structure. Radical feminism considers the male-controlled capitalist hierarchy as the defining feature of women's oppression. According to this group total uprooting and reconstruction of society is necessary. Conservative feminism is conservative relative to the society in which it is present. Libertarian feminism conceives people as self-owners and therefore being entitled to freedom from coercive interference. Separatist feminism does not support heterosexual relationships. Lesbian feminism is thus closely related. Other feminists criticize separatist feminism as sexist. Eco-feminists see men's control of land as responsible for the oppression of women and destruction of the natural environment.

Materialist ideologies:

Materialist feminisms grew out of Western Marxist thought and have inspired a number of different but overlapping movements. All of them are involved in a critique of capitalism and are focussed on their ideology's relationship with women. Marxist feminism argues that capitalism is the main source of women's oppression. According to them discrimination against women in domestic life and employment is an effect of capitalist ideologies. Socialist feminism distinguishes itself from Marxist feminism. They argue that women's liberation can only be achieved by working to end both the economic and cultural sources of women's oppression. According to Anarcha-feminists, class struggle and anarchy against the state require struggling against patriarchy, which comes from involuntary hierarchy.

Postcolonial ideologies:

Mostly during the course of history, the feminist movements and their theoretical developments were led predominantly by middle-class white women from Western Europe and North America. Women of other

races have however proposed alternative feminisms. This trend acceler-
ated in the 1960s with the civil rights movement in the United States and
the collapse of European colonialism. Since then, women in developing nations, former colonies, and those of diverse ethnicities or living
in poverty, have proposed additional feminisms. Womanism emerged
after early feminist movements that were largely white and middle-class.
Postcolonial feminists argue that colonial oppression and Western feminism marginalized postcolonial women but did not turn them passive or
voiceless. Third-world feminism is closely related to postcolonial feminism. These ideas also correspond with ideas in African feminism, moth-
erism, Stiwanism, negofeminism, femalism, transnational feminism, and
Africana womanism.

Social constructionist ideologies:

During the late twentieth century various feminists began to reason that
gender roles in a society are socially constructed, and that it is impossible to generalize women's experiences across cultures and histories.
According to them, if women or men are behaving in a particular manner in a society, than it is due to the social construction of that society.
Gender roles may be different in other parts of the world due to a different social construction. It also implies that the roles of women and
men that are generally found in this world are due to the social construct
therefore can be changed.

Cultural and visual arts movements:

Modern feminism also influenced the arts and culture in many parts
of the world. Riot grrrl is an underground feminist punk movement
that started in the 1990s. It was grounded in the DIY philosophy of
punk values. Riot grrls took an anti-corporate stance of self-sufficiency
and self-reliance. Riot grrrl's emphasis on universal female identity and
separatism often appears more closely allied with Second-wave feminism than with the Third-wave. The movement encouraged and made
'adolescent girls' standpoints central, allowing them to express themselves fully.

Lipstick feminism is a cultural feminist movement that attempts to respond to the backlash of second-wave radical feminism of the 1960s and 1970s by reclaiming symbols of 'feminine' identity such as make-up, suggestive clothing and having a sexual allure as valid and empowering personal choices.

The feminist art movement refers to the efforts of feminists to make art that reflects women's lives and experiences, as well as to change the foundation for the production and reception of contemporary art. It also sought to bring more visibility to women within art history and art practice.

FEMINISM AND SEX

A large variety of influential women during the 1970s accepted lesbianism and bisexuality as part of feminism. A significant proportion of feminists favoured this view, however, others considered sexuality irrelevant to the attainment of other goals. Sexual representation, sexuality, sadomasochism, the role of transwomen in the lesbian community, and other sexual issues resulted in bitter debates among feminists that are known as the feminist sex wars.

Opinions about the sex industry are diverse among feminists. Some are critical to it as they see it as exploitative, a result of patriarchal social structures and reinforcing sexual and cultural attitudes that are complicit in rape and sexual harassment. On the other hand some are supportive of at least parts of it and argue that some forms of it can be a medium of feminist expression and a means of women taking control of their sexuality. Some feminists are very much against pornography whereas others are not. Anti-prostitution feminists strongly oppose prostitution, as they see the practice as a form of violence against and exploitation of women, and a sign of male dominance over women. Other feminists hold that prostitution and other forms of sex work can be valid choices for women.

FEMINISM AND SCIENCE

Women's movement has inspired social scientists and biologists to raise critical questions about the ways traditional researchers have explained gender, sex and relations within and between the social and natural worlds. Some feminists criticize traditional scientific discourse as being historically biased towards a male perspective. A portion of the feminist research agenda is the examination of the ways in which power inequities are created and reinforced in scientific / academic institutions.

One criticism on feminist epistemology is that it allows political and social values to influence its findings. Some people also point out that feminist epistemology reinforces traditional stereotypes about women's thinking (as intuitive and emotional, etc.). (Epistemology is the branch of philosophy concerned with the nature and scope of knowledge. It questions what knowledge is, how it is acquired, and the possible extent a given subject or entity can be known.)

FEMINISM AND THEOLOGY

Feminist theology is a movement which reconsiders the traditions, practices, scriptures, and theologies of religions from a feminist point of view. Some of the objectives of feminist theology include increasing the role of women among the clergy and religious authorities, reinterpreting male-dominated imagery and language about God, determining women's place in relation to career and motherhood, and studying images of women in the religion's sacred texts.

Christian feminism seeks to interpret and understand Christianity in light of the equality of women and men, and assert that this interpretation is necessary for a complete understanding of Christianity. There is no standard set of beliefs among Christian feminists, however most of them agree that God does not discriminate on the basis of sex. They are involved in issues such as the ordination of women, male dominance and the balance of parenting in Christian marriage, claims of moral deficiency and inferiority of women compared to men, and the overall treatment of women in the church.

Jewish feminism seeks to improve the religious, legal, and social status of women within Judaism and to open up new opportunities for their religious experience and leadership. The main areas of work for early Jewish feminists in these movements were the exclusion from the all-male prayer group or minyan, the exemption from positive time-bound mitzvot, and women's inability to function as witnesses and to initiate divorce.

Secular / atheist feminists have engaged in criticism of religions. They argue that many religions have oppressive rules towards women and have misogynistic themes and elements in their religious texts.

Islamic feminists advocate women's rights, social justice and gender equality grounded within the Islamic framework. They highlight the deeply rooted teachings of equality in the Holy Quran and encourage a questioning of the patriarchal interpretation of Islamic teachings through the Quran, Hadith (sayings of Prophet Muhammad PBUH), and Sharia (law) towards the creation of a more equal and just society. The movement's pioneers have also utilized secular and Western feminist discourses and recognize the role of Islamic feminism as part of an integrated global feminist movement.

PATRIARCHY

Patriarchy is a term which is widely used and often condemned by most feminists. It is defined as a social system in which the role of the male as the primary authority figure is central to social organization, and where fathers hold authority over women, children, and property. It implies institutions of male rule and privilege and is therefore dependent on female subordination. Although there can be various levels of patriarchy in various regions of the world, most forms of feminism characterize patriarchy as an unjust social system that is oppressive to women. In feminist theory the concept of patriarchy often includes all the social mechanisms that reproduce and apply male dominance over women. Feminist theory typically characterizes patriarchy as a social construction, which can be overcome by critically analyzing and revealing its manifestations.

According to some radical feminists, patriarchy is too deeply rooted in societies therefore separatism is the only viable solution against it. Separatism is the advocacy of a state of cultural, ethnic, tribal, religious, racial, governmental or gender separation from the larger group. Separatist feminism is a form of radical feminism that holds that opposition to patriarchy is best done through focusing exclusively on women and girls. Some separatist feminists do not believe that men can make positive contributions to the feminist movement and that even well-intentioned, men replicate the dynamics of patriarchy. Many other feminists have criticized these radical feminist views as being anti-men.

The tension caused in society by Second-wave feminism gave rise to a backlash in the form of anti-feminist men's movements, such as Masculism or masculinism. It may refer to advocacy of the rights or needs of men and the adherence to or promotion of their opinions, values, etc., regarded as typical of men. Today many see masculism as a complementary movement that does not oppose feminism.

CONFLICTING VIEWS
ABOUT FEMINISM

Men and women both have been among the supporters and critics of modern feminism. They are termed as 'Pro-feminist' and 'Anti-feminists' respectively.

Pro-feminism:

Pro-feminism is the support of feminism without explicitly stating that the supporter is a member of the feminist movement. This term 'Pro-Feminism' is most often used in reference to men who are actively supportive of feminism. The actions of pro-feminist men's groups include anti-violence work with boys and young men in schools, offering sexual harassment workshops in workplaces, counselling male perpetrators of violence, running community education campaigns, etc. Such men are also involved in men's health, activism against pornography which includes anti-pornography legislation, men's studies, and the development of gender equity curricula in schools. They work sometimes in collaboration with feminists and women's services such as domestic violence and rape crisis centers.

Anti-feminism:

Anti-feminism is opposition to feminism in some or all of its forms. During the nineteenth century, anti-feminism was mainly focused on opposition to women's suffrage. In later years, opponents of women's entry into higher learning institutions argued that education was too great a physical burden on women. Others opposed women's entry into the labor force, or their right to join unions, to sit on juries, or to obtain birth control and control of their sexuality.

Some have opposed feminism on the grounds that they believe it is contrary to traditional values or religious beliefs. Anti-feminists argue, for example, that social acceptance of divorce and non-married women is wrong and harmful, and that males and females are fundamentally different and therefore their different traditional roles in society should be maintained. Others oppose women's entry into the workforce, political office, and the voting process, as well as the lessening of male authority in families.

Some people show extremist views against feminism. For example, Dr. Henry Makow, a Jewish writer in Canada and the inventor of the board-game Scruples, in his article 'Debauchery of American Womenhood' writes, "Feminism is another cruel New World Order hoax that has debauched American women and despoiled Western civilization." [3]

Rev. Pat Robertson in 1992 while offering his views on empowered women said, "Feminism is a socialist, anti-family political movement that encourages women to leave their husbands, kill their children, practice witchcraft, destroy capitalism and become lesbians." [4]

Many people oppose some forms of feminism, though they identify themselves as feminists. According to them, for example, feminism often promotes misandry (hatred or dislike of men/boys) and the elevation of women's interests above men's. They criticize radical feminist positions as harmful to both men and women.

Chapter 4

Equity Or Equality

*"We have to be careful in this era of radical feminism, not to empha-
size an equality of the sexes that leads women to imitate men to prove
their equality. To be equal does not mean you have to be the same."*

(Eva Evelyn Burrows, *Australian community welfare organizer)* [1]

While conducting training on the topic of Feminism to a group of women,
I asked a question to the participants, "Whenever a woman enters in a
bus and there is no unoccupied seat to sit, I usually stand up and offer
my seat to her and this is what most men do in the culture we live in.
What do you think about this practice?" Two women trainees asserted
that this is not right and is against the concept equality between men and
women. Then I asked the same two trainees, "There is a separate window
for women to facilitate them in the highly crowded office of NADRA
(National Database and Registration Authority of Pakistan) with long
queues of men. Is this right practice?" They immediately replied, this is
discrimination. They asserted that there should not be a separate window
for women as they are equal to men. According to them, women should
also stand in long queues just like men, waiting for their turn for hours.
Then I asked, "There are separate toilets for men and women. Is this
right?" There was a moment of silence followed by a reply that this is
right. When asked, "Where is the equality now?" The reply was, "Toilets
are also separate in the Western countries". This reasoning of theirs was
however not acceptable to me. Right behaviour does not depend on
whether it is practiced in the East or the West. Right is right no matter
where it is practiced.

If it were their reply that even the toilets should be the same, then
I would have asked, "Should men and women fight with each other
in the WWE wrestling bouts?" Or, "Will you like to accept a hand-
wrestling challenge with men?" But their philosophy of perfect equality between the two sexes vanished well before reaching such extreme
questions.

ARE MEN AND WOMEN SIMILAR?

"Are men and women similar?" The answer to this question by any logical and scientific person would be "No" as there are many differences between the two sexes. There are, however, some women who wish to deny the existence of such differences or do not want to discuss them. There is a particular reason behind such behaviour as mentioned by Tamara McClintock Greenberg, Psy.D., M.S., a clinical psychologist, in her article 'Differences between men and women: Talking about Inequalities in the Shadow of the Feminist Movement':

"Talking openly about the biological differences between men and women can be complicated. Louann Brizendine, M.D. wrote a bestselling book in 2006 about the way male and female brains and bodies differ. Whatever readers or reviewers thought about the book, it has been translated into 30 languages and obviously speaks to something we women are concerned about, which is talking about how men and women are different. Of course, socialization and the way we are raised plays an important role, but biology does seem to matter. This may not be news to young women and men, but for women in Brizendine's generation and my own, such talk can feel like heresy. Brizendine brings this up in the epilogue of her book: 'There are those who wish there were no differences between men and women. In the 1970's at the University of California, Berkeley, the buzzword among young women was 'mandatory unisex', which meant that it was politically incorrect even to mention sex difference.'"

"Something curious happened along the way for women exposed to feminist beliefs. Those of us in our 40's and beyond were reared in a time in which we felt we had to deny differences between the sexes. This message had a purpose. We had to justify equal rights and equal pay. Although I can't say that we have really achieved either, it certainly is better than it has been, at least in the United States. Yet, our current state of external inequality makes it harder to talk about internal and biological differences. Brizendine goes on to say, 'The fear of discrimination based on difference runs deep, and for many years assumptions about sex differences went scientifically unexamined for fear that women wouldn't be able to claim equality with men.'" [2]

Women were especially worried about the differences in the brain as acknowledged by Jill Becker, a psychologist at the University of Michigan, "In the early '80s, we were worried that sex differences in the brain would be used against us as women." [3] Psychologists Julian Stanley and Camilla Benbow, in 1980, ignited a firestorm when they proposed that gifted boys did better at mathematics than gifted girls because of a 'math gene'. The nature vs. nurture debate continued, but it is becoming more pragmatic as researchers use MRIs and other brain-imaging tools that show differences in male and female brains even when performance is identical. [4]

There are many physical as well as psychological differences between men and women. As I mentioned in Chapter 1 of this book, there is nothing wrong with women if they are different from men. In fact this is part of their feminine beauty. And similarly for men it is part of their beauty to be masculine and to be different from women. Both sexes are important and wonderful creations of the Almighty God.

In order to have a understanding of the differences between the two sexes, I am reproducing a very good article by Ms. Heidi who is LDN (licensed dietician-nutritionist) and works as a Clinical Dietician in Philadelphia. Following is her article:

DIFFERENCE BETWEEN MALE AND FEMALE STRUCTURES [5]

Over the years there have been many arguments and studies relating to this subject and, although some gender differences are proven and some still controversial, they should not be confused with sexist stereotypes. No one can really tell whether these gender differences are caused by nature or environment-learned, but the fact is that some amount of sex differentiation takes place immediately as the male or female begins to develop within the womb.

Some differences (such as reproductive organs) are congenital, while others obviously environmental (such as given names). Contrary to the beliefs of feminists or bisexuals, several studies have proven that there are expressed differences between males and females programmed within the DNA from the moment of conception.

Physical differences:

There are several obvious differences between men and women, including the following:

1. *An average man is taller and heavier than an average woman.*
2. *Men have more bodily hair than women do, especially on the chest and extremities*
3. *Women are more sensitive to sound than men*
4. *Men are over 30% stronger than women, especially in the upper body. Although many feminists cannot face this fact, females simply do not have the strength or endurance necessary to be, for example, effective combat soldiers.*
5. *On average, girls begin puberty changing approximately two years before boys.*
6. *Men have larger hearts and lungs, and their higher levels of testosterone cause them to produce greater amounts of red blood cells*
7. *Differences in intake and delivery of oxygen translate into some aspects of performance: when a man is jogging at about 50% of his capacity, a woman will need to work at over 70% of her capacity to keep up with him.*
8. *Female fertility decreases after age 35, ending with menopause, but men are capable of making children even when very old.*
9. *Men's skin has more collagen and sebum, which makes it thicker and oilier than women's skin*
10. *Women generally have a greater body fat percentage than men.*
11. *Men and women have different levels of certain hormones; for example, men have a higher concentration of androgens such as testosterone, while women have a higher concentration of estrogens.*
12. *An average male brain has approximately 4% more cells and 100 grams more brain tissue than an average female brain. This is not connected with*

intelligence! Research points to no overall difference in intelligence between males and females. However, both sexes have similar brain weight to body weight ratios.

13. *In men, the second digit is often shorter than the fourth digit, while in females the second tends to be longer than the fourth*
14. *Men have better distance vision and depth perception, and usually better vision in lighted environments. Women have better night vision, see better at the red end of the light spectrum, and have better visual memory.*

Diseases:-
1. *More men than women become infected with HIV.*
2. *More males are likely to be diagnosed with tuberculosis then females.*
3. *Women are less likely to suffer from cardiovascular disease.*
4. *Men are more likely to suffer from cancer.*
5. *Women are more likely to suffer from osteoarthritis, osteoporosis and blindness*

Mental differences:

Brain differences:- *Several studies have proven significant differences between male and female brains. Differences are located in both the primitive regions, and the newer parts of the brain called neocortex – the higher brain regions.*

Men and women process information differently because of differences in a portion of the brain called the splenium, which is much larger in women than in men, and has more brain-wave activity.

Intelligence:- *Many small-scale studies report differences not repeated in larger studies which, of course, caused much arguments and confusions. Several researches done on volunteers have proven that there is no significant difference in the average intelligence level of men and women. However, there are some slight differences:*

1. *An average man performs better on tests of spatial and mathematical ability, while women perform better on tests of verbal ability and memory.*
2. *Men's IQ has greater variance, which means that there are more men than women in the very high and very low IQ groups.*

Behavioral differences:- There are some proven behavioral differences between men and women and the most common are:

1. _Men are more physically aggressive._
2. _Men masturbate more._
3. _Women are less likely to successfully commit suicide, but more likely to attempt it._
4. _Men have more positive attitudes about sex than women do._
5. _Men are more prone to taking risks._
6. _Women express their emotions more readily and experience a greater intensity of emotion._

Differences in mental health:-

Several mental illnesses are proven to be differently distributed between genders.

The most common include:

1. _Depression – Several researches have shown that this disease affects females twice as often as it does males. Serotonin is a chemical required in the brain for "happy mood maintenance". The rate of synthesis and level of serotonin in the blood are significantly higher in men than in women. These differences may help explain why depression is more common in women. Both depression and panic disorder rates, which are two disorders with higher rates in women than men, may be tied to childhood experiences of abuse._
2. _Schizophrenia - Although this disorder affects men and women equally, men typically experience symptoms earlier, with more intensity, and have poorer prognosis than women. Symptoms of schizophrenia in women more frequently involve depression and greater disorders in thought conceptualization, while men report more apathy, disorders of speech, disturbance in cognitive function, and social isolation._
3. _Alzheimer's disease - Several studies have shown that women are at a higher risk of developing Alzheimer's disease than men are. This disease is caused by the damage to the white brain matter. On the other hand, men with Alzheimer's disease have a higher risk of mortality than women do._

4. *Stress Disorders - Anxiety disorders are chronic illnesses that occur more often in women than men. The risk of post-traumatic stress disorder following some traumatic experience is much higher in women than men. Women are also more likely to have been previously assaulted or to have sustained injury by a relative or someone known to them.*

5. *Happiness - In general, it has been proven that women are happier with their lives than men are. Women also show greater concern about family and home life issues, while men express more sympathies about political issues.*

6. *Different brains – different abilities: The difference between the male and female brain is not evidence of intelligence, unintelligence, superiority, or inferiority, but of field specializations. In general, males have better spatial and math skills than females. On the other hand, girls tend to be more vocal than boys. Males are much better in visualizing a three-dimensional object than women are.*

7. *Some other differences - life success, education, employment...*

Employment:- In most countries, there are more wealthy or rich men than there are women. There are much more unemployed females, as well. Employed women earn 80% of the income of men. Women are less productive then men – women in nonagricultural industries work 35.9 hours per week versus 41.6 hours for men.

More men work in the following industries:

- *Mining*
- *Construction*
- *Transportation*
- *Farming*
- *Computer and mathematical occupations*
- *Engineering and architecture.*
- *Chief executives*
- *Firefighters*
- *Police and patrol officers*

- *Electricians*
- *Dentists and surgeons.*

Women are far more likely than men to be:

- *Social workers*
- *Paralegals and legal assistants*
- *Teachers*
- *Nurses*
- *Speech pathologists*
- *Dental hygienists*
- *Maids and housekeeping cleaners*
- *Childcare workers.*

Education:- When talking about literacy we should keep in mind that, worldwide, men are more likely to be literate, with 100 men considered literate for every 88 women. Regarding high education, the differences are not so obvious. For example, women made up 57% of all college students in the United States, 58% in UK and 60% in Iran.

Internet usage:- The percentage of men using the Internet was ahead of the percentage of women, at least in United States where the study was conducted.

Men

- *Log on more often onto the net,*
- *Spend more time online,*
- *Download more music and videos,*
- *Are more likely to use the Internet to pay bills,*
- *Are more likely to be broadband users.*

Women

- *Are more likely to e-mail friends and family about a variety of topics*
- *Use the Internet for shopping and banking. (Article by Ms. Heidi)*

HYPOCRISY OF SOME PEOPLE

Some people or groups publically say that they believe in equality of the two sexes but their actions are quite contrary. I would call it hypocrisy. I am giving two examples, one from my country and the other from a developed European nation.

I was involved in conducting a series of trainings arranged for UNDP in collaboration with the Sindh Government for planning officers on the topic of 'Gender Sensitive Project Planning Skills'. These trainings were a part of a joint venture project between UNDP and the Government of Pakistan by the name of 'Gender Based Governance Systems (GBG).' Addressing the opening ceremony of the trainings, my boss (head of our training institute) asserted that men and women are equal. Women should also be involved in all the activities that men do. However after a few trainings, his standing orders were that no female faculty will teach in these trainings as the trainees, mostly men, were very crude and uncouth. However he continued to address the opening sessions with the same words as before.

Take another example of hypocrisy from a developed nation. It was portrayed by a world renowned automotive assembler that their assembly plant in UK is such that women can work at each and every work station [6]. Once a lady was asked to work at a workstation that required lot of physical exertion. She refused to work on that work station. When insisted, she gave a medical reason that this workstation is not suitable for women. The company was now in a dilemma. If they accept the woman's reasoning then their image as a gender friendly plant was in jeopardy. After much deliberation, the management decided that they will keep on publically portraying their plant as gender friendly; however there was an internal understanding within the plant that women will not be asked to work on that particular workstation. This is hypocrisy.

THE CONCEPT OF GENDER EQUITY

From the preceding discussion it is very much clear that the phenom-enon of equating men to women by some radical feminists is not sup-ported by scientific data. In fact equating men to women is harmful to both men and women.

World bodies have therefore defined gender equality in terms of human rights, especially women's rights and economic development. UNICEF describes gender equality as, "means that women and men, and girls and boys, enjoy the same rights, resources, opportunities and protections. It does not require that girls and boys, or women and men, be the same, or that they be treated exactly alike." [7] According to this definition, the con-cept of gender equality does not require that girls and boys, or women and men, be the same, or that they be treated exactly alike'. The two sexes are not the same and they therefore should be treated according to their respective characteristics and needs.

The term 'gender equity' is better than the term 'gender equality', although the two terms are interchangeably used by some and are not well understood even by some feminists. The concept of equity does not always require equal numbers of both sexes everywhere but requires equal recognition of the works being done by the two sexes. It does not mean to make the two sexes same but it means to highlight and value similarities and differences. It does not require equal inputs from both sexes but ensure equal outcomes.

UNDP training manual on gender issues takes the help of a few pic-tures to clear the concept of 'gender equity' [8]. The pictures are of a girl who is trying to feed soup to her two pets, a stork and a cat. The first picture shows that both the animals are given soup in glasses by the girl. The stork was able to drink the soup with the help of his long beak but the cat remained hungry as the glass did not serve her need. The second picture shows both animals being served soup in normal plates. This scheme also failed as the stork remained hungry as the plate was not appropriate for him. But this time the cat was able to feed herself.

The third picture shows soup being served based on the needs of the two animals. Stork was served soup in a glass and the cat was served soup in a plate. Contrary to the first two cases, the third case was based on the needs of two different animals and therefore resulted in the well being of both. Both stork and the cat were able to have soup very easily. This is the concept of equity that is to serve every one according to their respective needs which may require treating people differently.

Take another example. Suppose you have two children, a girl and a boy with different food intake needs. The concept of equity would require giving them food according their needs. If the girl wants to eat less then she should not be forced to eat more to match the boy's food intake. And in the same way, if the boy wants to eat less, then he should not be forced to eat more to match the girl. Each one should be provided food on the basis of their respective requirement. If we will give exactly the same quantity of food to the children, then one will remain hungry and the other can suffer from indigestion due to overeating. The concept of equity requires feeding appropriate quantity of food to the two children according to their needs which may be not equal.

Men and women are different and therefore their needs may vary. According to the concept of equity, these needs should be recognized and fulfilled. If in some aspect, women's needs are more than those of men's, for example healthcare, then they should be facilitated accordingly. Many diseases are common among men and women and therefore can be treated by the same doctors. However, there is a complete set of additional healthcare needs for women related to pregnancy and childbirth. Therefore allocating more budgets for women's health by the government is totally acceptable and based on the concept of gender equity.

The radical concept of strict equality between the two sexes is harmful to both men and women. According to Louann Brizendine, M.D, writer of the bestselling book in 2006 about the way male and female brains and bodies differ, "…pretending that women and men are the same, while doing a disservice to both men and women, ultimately hurts women." [9] Women cannot compete with men by becoming men.

They are different therefore their needs are different. As quoted earlier, according to Dr. Henry Makow, a Jewish anti-feminist writer, "Feminism teaches woman that feminine nature has resulted in 'oppression' and that she should convert to male behavior instead. The result: a confused and aggressive woman with a large chip on her shoulder, unfit to become a wife or mother." [10]

At the end of this chapter, for further elaborating the concept of gender equity, I am reproducing here an article by Ms. Lara David, a writer from USA, which explains the concept of gender equity and differentiates it with the concept of equality. Following is her article:

THE DIFFERENCE BETWEEN 'EQUITY' AND 'EQUALITY' [11]

Pay attention, folks, because this lesson is important. It's important for feminism, for humanity, for respect and tolerance. So read closely, because I don't get this fired up over nothing.

There's this activity I do in my class. All the students sit in a circle, and I ask everyone to take off his or her left shoe and throw it into a pile in the center. Once the shoes are all piled up, I begin re-distributing them, one to each student, completely at random. Then I tell everyone to put on the new shoes. And inevitably, there begin the complaints.

"This isn't my shoe!"

"It's too big!"

"It's too small!"

"This doesn't fit me!"

Whatever the specific complaints are, very few students are actually happy with their newly mismatched pair of shoes. "What's wrong?" I ask. "I did everything fairly. You all have two shoes - one for your right foot and one for your left."

"But Miss David," they say, "they aren't the correct shoes!"

"Oh," I say. "You want the shoes that are best for each of you individually? Not just any shoe I find?"

"Yes!" they all say.

"But," I say, with furrowed brow, "that doesn't seem fair. I wanted to treat you all EQUALLY." I point to a boy with somewhat large feet, and a nearby girl with smallish feet. "He'll have more shoe than you will," I note. And without a doubt, someone unknowingly gets right to the heart of the issue:

"It doesn't matter who has more shoe, Miss David. It matters that we all have the right shoes for us."

And THAT, my friends, is the difference between equity and equality. Equality means everyone gets exactly the same outcome - two shoes - without regard to individual differences - large or small feet, for example. Equity means everyone gets the same quality of outcome - shoes that fit their individual needs.

A lot of feminist arguments are either poorly worded, claiming to desire equality for women in situations where they would actually prefer equity, or misunderstood as demanding equality when they are, in fact, demanding equity. This has become remarkably apparent to me in the recent barrage of posts about women bloggers and how they earn - or fail to earn - respect for their work. Catherine wrote this in her MamaPop post:

What is radical about it is that we push on, demanding to be heard, and demanding recognition of our worth as mothers, women, writers, business-people, innovators, people, against the ignorance of those who would keep us down.

Some have interpreted this as a half-hearted and hypocritical demand for equality, when it is actually anything but. Demanding recognition as mothers and women sort of fundamentally requires an expectation that we will not be treated exactly the same as a man would. Why would we want to be treated exactly like men anyway? In case you didn't notice, WE'RE NOT MEN. What we're demanding is not equality - it's equity.

We demand respect for doing a damn hard job and doing it well. We demand respect for creating a community that inspires and uplifts in the face of some of life's greatest challenges. We demand respect for refusing to compromise our femininity in the face of professional obstacles. We don't demand the EXACT SAME RESPECT that men receive - that's like demanding everyone wear the same shoes, regardless of size. We demand the respect that is most fitting to our stations, but damn it, we still demand the respect. We are women, and we should be treated as women - to do otherwise would be to ignore plain facts. But being treated as women should not automatically mean being treated as less serious or less important, and that's the problem with having an article about our work in the field of blogging - which really is primarily a technological field - placed in the "Style" section of the New York Times.

We are not screaming our heads off to be placated with promises of equality. We are not men - do not treat us as men. We are women, and we demand equity. (Article by Ms. Lara David)

Chapter 5
Liberation Or Debauchery

"The ancient Greek philosophers argued whether or not woman had a soul. But the civilized West has settled the question once for all. The woman is nothing but body. That is why we see her semi-clad and nude pictures on every square inch of available space at a time when the West is busy congratulating itself for the remarkable progress of its women."

(Khalid Baig, *Pakistani writer and editor of Albalagh magazine)* [1]

DEBAUCHERY OF THE SOCIETY

As mentioned in Chapter 3 of this book, a large variety of Western influential women during the 1970s accepted lesbianism and bisexuality as part of feminism. A significant proportion of feminists favoured this view, however others considered it irrelevant to the attainment of other goals. Sexual representation, sexuality, sadomasochism, the role of transwomen in the lesbian community, and other sexual issues started bitter feminist debates that are known as the 'feminist sex wars'.

Many present day so called 'liberal' women tend to portray their liberty and modernism by their immodest dressing. One wonders why the idea of women liberation today is so closely linked by some with the idea of liberation from clothes. If nudity is the sign of modernization then the people shown in the famous old movie 'One Million Years B.C' were the most progressive and modern. This also implies that a donkey of his time was more progressive than Sir Albert Einstein because the former was not fond of using the clothes.

Yvonne Ridley is British journalist, war correspondent and Respect Party politician who converted to Islam from Christianity. She in one of her articles writes, "We hate those ghastly beauty pageants, and tried to stop laughing in 2003 when judges of the Miss Earth competition hailed the emergence of a bikini-clad Miss Afghanistan, Vida Samadzai, as a giant leap for women's liberation. They even gave Samadzai a special award for 'representing the victory of women's rights.' ….. What is more liberating: being judged on the length of your skirt and the size of your surgically enhanced breasts, or being judged on your character and intelligence?" [2]

This so called process of liberty also happened in many other countries. Mr. Aftab Ahmed Shamsi, a Pakistani writer and intellectual, mentions this process in his words:

"…1975 was an important year for the women liberation. Even in Pakistan this year was very well celebrated. Many seminars were arranged and editorials were written. Local movie producers also showed women with more freedom. Movie theatres started to show 'blue' movies of the foreign completely liberated ladies. Some people fully supported women liberty by damaging the theatre seats and theatre screens because women were not shown fully liberated (from clothes).

This liberty was earned by women in a long journey. Initially she used to be behind the veil within her homes, and men used to sit outside their homes in a 'charpai' (eastern low cost traditional bed) wearing only 'tah-band' (a short cloth wrapped across the waist) and smoking a 'huqqa'. With the passage of time, women got rid of veils and men preferred for themselves 'shalwar' suits / pant shirts and to sit in the drawing rooms.

Time passed and the world learnt more about liberty and rights. The world took another step towards freedom. Sleeve-less, and see-through clothing became popular among women. On the other hand, coats, socks, and hats became popular among men.

Time passed on. In the third phase towards liberty and rights, women preferred to wear topless and hipster dresses in formal parties. Make-up was performed on each and every part of the body to display her freedom. A lot of time was consumed for this display. On the other hand three-piece suits became popular among men.

The women living inside their homes thought that the freedom from dress is necessary for individual freedom and on the other hand men kept on going inside the layers of clothes. The battle for liberty continued..." [3]

Dr. Henry Makow, a Jewish writer in Canada and the inventor of the board-game Scruples, in his article 'Debauchery of American Womenhood' writes:

".......the bikinied American beauty queen struts practically naked in front of millions on TV. A feminist, she belongs to herself. In practice, paradoxically, she is public property. She belongs to no one and everyone. She shops her body to the highest bidder. She is auctioning herself all of the time.

In America, the cultural measure of a woman's value is her sex appeal. (As this asset depreciates quickly, she is neurotically obsessed with appearance and plagued by weight problems.)

As an adolescent, her role model is Britney Spears, a singer whose act approximates a strip tease. From Britney, she learns that she will be loved only if she gives sex. Thus, she learns to 'hook up' furtively rather than to demand patient courtship, love and marriage. As a result, dozens of males know her before her husband does. She loses her innocence, which is a part of her charm. She becomes hardened and calculating. Unable to love, she is unfit to receive her husband's seed.

...In the 'brave new world', women are not supposed to be mothers and progenitors of the race. They are meant to be neutered, autonomous sex objects.

Liberating women is often given as an excuse for the war in Afghanistan. Liberating them to what? To Britney Spears? To low-rise 'see-my-thong' pants? To the mutual masturbation that passes for sexuality in America? If they really cared about women, maybe they'd end the war.

Parenthood is the pinnacle of human development. It is the stage when we finally graduate from self-indulgence and become God's surrogates: creating and nurturing new life. The New World Order does not want us to reach this level of maturity. Pornography is the substitute for marriage. We are to remain single: stunted, sex-starved and self-obsessed.

We are not meant to have a permanent 'private' life. We are meant to remain lonely and isolated, in a state of perpetual courtship, dependent on consumer products for our identity.

This is especially destructive for woman. Her sexual attraction is a function of her fertility. As fertility declines, so does her sex appeal. If a woman devotes her prime years to becoming 'independent', she is not likely to find a permanent mate.

Her long-term personal fulfillment and happiness lies in making marriage and family her first priority." [4]

Negative effects on society:

This debauchery of society produced many social evils like increased divorce rates, increased single parent families, neglected children, sexual exploitation, objectification, unwanted pregnancies, and the spread of AIDS and other sexually transmitted diseases (STDs). As this topic is vast and complex, I will discuss only a few points here, starting with the unwanted pregnancies.

According to New Mexico School of Medicine, "One million teens in the USA will become pregnant over the next twelve months. Ninety-five percent of those pregnancies are unintended. About one-third will end in abortion; one third will end in spontaneous miscarriage; and one third will continue their pregnancy to term & keep their baby. More than half of them are 17 years old or younger when they have their first pregnancy. The poorer the young woman, the more likely she will become a mother.

Almost half of all teen mothers end up on welfare. Less than 25 percent of births to teens occur within wedlock". [5]

According to the newspaper daily Mail of UK: "Nearly a quarter of all abortions in Britain are carried out on girls under the age of 20, a major report has revealed…The data, compiled by the REPROSTAT group, the EU's community health monitoring programme, details abortion figures across the region. Most of the figures are for 2008, but the data is slightly older for several countries. The report shows some 1.2 million terminations are carried out a year – the equivalent of the populations of member countries Malta & Cyprus combined." [6]

Early pregnancies cause many negative affects in a society including negative health effects on teen parents including anaemia, hypertension, obesity, STDs, negative effects on children, and negative effects on the society.

According to US department of Health and Human Service, teen girls who have babies are; less likely to finish high school, more likely to rely on public assistance, more likely to be poor as adults, and more likely to have children who have poorer educational, behavioural, and health outcomes over the course of their lives than do kids born to older parents. Teen childbearing costs U.S. taxpayers billions of dollars due to lost tax revenue, increased public assistance payments, and greater expenditures for public health care, foster care, and criminal justice services. [7]

High divorce rate is becoming another social problem in many countries including the developed countries. In the United States, researchers estimate that 40%–50% of all first marriages, and 60% of second marriages, will end in divorce. [8]

Dr. Hawkins, Ph.D, has been a member of the faculty in the School of Family Life at Brigham Young University since 1990. He is chair of the Utah Commission on Marriage, which advises the state on its efforts to help couples form and sustain healthy marriages. He has worked with the federal government in its efforts to explore ways to strengthen marriages in US society. He is also an advisor to the National Center for Marriage Research at Bowling Green State University, the National Center for African American Marriages and Families at Hampton University, and a member of the Texas Healthy Marriage Initiative Research Advisory Group. He was the research hub director of the National Healthy Marriage Resource Center. He has published dozens of scholarly articles and three books on marriage, divorce, and fathering. Dr. Hawkins in his book 'Should keep trying to work it out?' writes, "There are some well known factors that put people at higher risk for divorce: marrying at a very early age, less education and income, living together before marriage, a premarital pregnancy, no religious affiliation, coming from a divorced family, and feelings of insecurity." [9]

Please note that some reasons mentioned for the high divorce rate are living together before marriage, premarital pregnancy, and no religious affiliation. Regarding the Western practice of living together he writes, "Couples who live together before marriage appear to have a much higher chance of divorce if they marry. However, this risk is mostly for those who live together with more than one partner. ...The idea that living together before marriage increases your risk for divorce goes against a lot of common beliefs that it is a good way to get to know each other better and prepare for marriage." [10]

Regarding premarital childbearing, he writes, "Pregnancy and childbearing prior to marriage significantly increase the likelihood of future divorce. In America, more than one-third (37%) of children are born to parents who are not married, and few of these parents eventually marry. Most of those parents will separate before the child begins school, and some will never really get together." [11]

Regarding religious affiliation, he writes, "Researchers have estimated that individuals who report belonging to some religious group have a somewhat lower chance of divorce than those who say they have no religious affiliation. And if couples share the same religious affiliation, their chances of divorce are even lower." [12]

Single parenting is also another problem that has arisen in modern Western societies. Single parenting has become an accepted norm in the United States and is an accepted trend found in multiple other countries. Although divorce is one of the main events that lead to single parenting, it may be that the majority of cases (in the US) are from pregnancy outside of wedlock. In the United States, 72.6% of single parents are mothers. Among this percentage of single mothers: 45% of single mothers are currently divorced or separated, 1.7% are widowed, and 34% of single mothers never have been married. [13]

Children raised by one parent are more likely to display serious behaviour problems, according to research mentioned in the British newspaper Telegraph. According to this research children raised by single mothers are twice as likely to misbehave as those born into traditional two-parent families. According to Lisa Calderwood from London University's Institute of Education, "Living apart from natural fathers can be associated with poverty and negative outcomes for children." [14]

Thus, as evident from the preceding facts and figures, there are many problems that have arisen in the societies that have gone away from morality.

SEX INDUSTRY

There are diverse opinions among the feminists regarding the sex industry. Some are critical to it as they see it as exploitative and others are supportive, to at least parts of it. Donna M. Hughes is a professor in women studies program in the University of Rhode Island. Following are some excerpts of the lecture on sexual exploitation by Donna M. Hughes depicting the harms brought by prostitution:

Prostitution and Trafficking for Sexual Exploitation:

Prostitution is not the world's oldest profession, as is commonly said, although it is probably one of the world's oldest forms of men's violence against women and girls. It seems old because men's sexual exploitation of women and children is ancient and defended as a part of men's natures that they have to have sex, even if it is purchased, forced or with a child. Prostitution is not natural or inevitable; it is abuse and exploitation of women and girls that results from structural inequality between women and men on a world scale. Prostitution commodifies women and girls and markets their bodies for whatever acts men have sexualized and want to buy. Rarely are adult men treated this way.

The majority of girls enter prostitution before they have reached the age of consent. Each year for the past decade, the average age of girls in prostitution has declined, especially in Asia and Africa where men have created a demand for young girls, assuming they are free of HIV. Girls are sold into prostitution by relatives. Pimps recruit them after they run away from home. They enter prostitution after enduring incest, abuse and rape by acquaintances, which accommodates them to violence and exploitation until eventually they think this is their role in life.

Poverty, desperation to support family members, and drug addictions compel women into prostitution. When the social infrastructure collapses as a result of war, famine, and economic crisis women turn to prostitution as a last resort.

No matter how women and girls get into prostitution, it is difficult to get out. Pimps and brothel owners use violence, threats, and addictions to drugs and alcohol to control the woman, sometimes keeping them in slavery-like conditions. Often women can leave prostitution only after they are used-up, become ill, and no longer make money for the pimps. Women in prostitution are further burdened with a stigmatized identity that is impossible to escape, unless their pasts are kept a secret.

There is no dignity in prostitution. Many of the acts of prostitution, including those that are photographed in the making of pornography, are intended to degrade, humiliate and express domination over women. They are acts of misogyny, not respect or affection, and have nothing to do with love or intimacy. Women don't emerge from sexual exploitation into positions of power, respect or admiration. They remain powerless as individuals and an underclass as a group.

Most laws aimed at suppressing prostitution are based on the sexually repressive doctrines of patriarchal religions that view prostitution as immoral activity, with women being the most immoral participants. In this view, men give in to the temptation offered by immoral women. Men have traditionally condemned prostitution in public, while ensuring its continuation in private. Where prostitution is illegal, it is usually the women who are punished; pimps, traffickers, and men who buy women in prostitution are seldom punished. Being bought, sold and enslaved in prostitution is a condition for which women and children can be arrested, imprisoned, deported, and sometimes executed.

Trafficking is the practice that delivers women and children into sexual exploitation. The number of women trafficked for this purpose is unknown, although conservative estimates put the number in the millions. Women do not voluntarily put themselves in situations where they are exploited, beaten, raped and enslaved. Women do not traffic themselves. Criminals who recruit, buy and sell women and girls are the crucial intermediaries for delivering women into prostitution. Traffickers supply the necessary elements for travel, such as money, documents, and connections in other countries. Traffickers are paid a sum of money for each woman and girl they deliver to a brothel or pimp. They use force, coercion, seduction, deception, and any other techniques that are effective in controlling the women and girls they are trading.

Criminals traffic women and girls within borders, from rural areas to cities, and from town to town on circuits to provide new faces and bodies to men who want variety. They traffic them to large sex industry centers for men's nightlife entertainment, to migrant labor camps for men's hometown comfort, and to immigrant communities to provide sex for men who want women from their own nationality. They traffic them to rural areas for farmers who want wives, and to the US, Australia and Western Europe for men who want non-feminist wives.

Global Sexual Exploitation--Supply and Demand Markets:

Prostitution and trafficking in women and children are global phenomena. They occur all over the world and the activities are carried out transnationally. There is a global culture of sexual exploitation in which women's bodies are used to market consumer products and where women and girls themselves are products to be consumed. Currently, the global sex industry is estimated to make US$52 billion dollars a year. To keep the sex industry in business, women are trafficked to, from and through every region in the world. The value of this global trade in women as commodities for sex industries is estimated to be between seven and twelve billion dollars annually.

The global sexual exploitation of women and girls is a supply and demand market. Men create the demand and women are the supply. Cities and countries where men's demand for women in prostitution is legalized or tolerated are the receiving sites, while countries and areas where traffickers easily recruit women are the sending regions.

Sending countries or regions are characterized by poverty, unemployment, war, and political and economic instability. These conditions facilitate the activity of traffickers who target regions where recruiting victims is easy. In sending countries, such as Vietnam, the rise of consumerism has led families to accept loans for material goods from traffickers in exchange for the use of their daughters. In many parts of Asia, daughters are culturally bound to repay their families for their upbringing, and a daughter in the sex industry is sometimes the main financial support for families in impoverished areas. Women and girls become vulnerable to traffickers as a result of family pressure, poverty, family violence, and community conflicts. Traffickers procure women and girls when their families say, 'Go', or when women say to themselves, 'Anything is better than this'.

In receiving countries or sites where men's demand for women and girls in prostitution exceeds the supply in the local area, women and girls must be recruited and imported. Sex industries use up women, physically and emotionally, necessitating fresh supplies of women, which keeps the trafficking of women so profitable.

Criminals and organized crime groups have always been the organizers and money-makers of the sex industry. In the United States, they were the founders and controllers of the pornography industry for decades. Sex industries contribute to secondary illegal activity, such as money laundering, which is needed to convert illegal cash into useable funds. The criminal networks that traffic women are fully transnational. Some are composed of a few loosely connected individuals, while others are highly organized crime syndicates, such as the Mafia, the Yakuza, Triads and 'Russian' crime groups.

The Internet has become a site for the global sexual exploitation of women and children. In the past five years, sex industries have been the leaders in opening up the Internet for business. The Internet is almost without regulation because its international reach has made local and national laws and standards either obsolete or unenforceable. In addition, governments, such as the United States, decided on a 'hands-off' policy to allow the sex industry almost unfettered operation on the Internet. With new types of technology, pornographers have introduced new ways to exploit and abuse women. With the techniques of videoconferencing, live sex shows are broadcast in which men dictate the performances of the women.

In 1999, the revenue from pornography and live sex shows on the Internet was US$1 billion dollars and comprised 69 percent of the Internet content sales. Pornographers in the United States garnered a majority of the money.

Intense competition on the Internet has led pornographers to attract buyers with more extreme images, such as bondage, torture, bestiality and child pornography, leading to increased violence against women and children as more degrading and violent images, videos and live performances are made and marketed. Last year, an American in Phnom Penh, Cambodia set up a live video chat site to broadcast the pay-per-view rape and torture of women.

The Harm of Sexual Exploitation – From the Individual to the State:

Global sexual exploitation is a human rights crisis for women and girls. It is also a crisis for democracy and the security of nations. The harm of sexual exploitation extends from the individual to the state.

The rape-like sex acts of prostitution cause harm to women and girls' bodies and minds. Women contract sexually transmitted and other infectious diseases, such as tuberculosis. They suffer from post-traumatic stress, depression and anxiety. Under these conditions women make the best choices they can. Rarely do these choices approach true consent. With few options, women comply in hope that eventually they will earn enough money to buy their way out of debt bondage or find a way to escape. When escape is not possible, they use drugs and alcohol to numb themselves from the emotional distress and assaults to their dignity and bodily integrity. Most women and girls emerge from prostitution ill, traumatized, and as poor as when they entered. For increasing numbers of women and girls, prostitution is a death sentence when they contract HIV. In some regions, more than fifty percent of prostituted women have HIV/AIDS.

The sex industry targets and consumes young women, usually under age 25. When a state permits prostitution or trafficking to flourish a certain portion of each generation of young women will be lost. Some might argue that prostitution is the work of women, a way of making a living unique to their gender, but in fact, prostitution is the position the dominant class puts the subordinate class into, in order to use them as they desire. Prostitution creates an underclass of women whose purpose is to sexually serve men. It is a degraded status, everywhere. No form of sexual exploitation leads to the liberation or empowerment of women, or enhances the rights or status of women.

Prostitution and trafficking are extreme forms of gender discrimination and exist as a result of the powerlessness of women as a class. Sexual exploitation is more than an act; it is a systematic way to abuse and control women that socializes and coerces women and girls until they comply, take ownership of their own subordinate status, and say, 'I choose this'.

Prostitution and trafficking restrict women's freedom and citizenship rights. If women are treated as commodities, they are consigned to second-class citizenship. No state can be a true democracy, if half of its citizens can potentially be treated as commodities.

In addition to harming the individual and creating an underclass of women, trafficking and prostitution operate through criminal activity and corruption that threaten the stability and security of nations. Due to relatively low risk and high profits, the trade in women is increasingly replacing the trade in drugs and arms as the preferred activity of transnational criminal networks. When officials are bribed or collaborate, they use their authority to protect criminals and profit from the sexual exploitation of women. As the influence of criminal networks on law enforcement and governments deepens, the corruption goes beyond occasionally ignoring illegal activity to providing protection by blocking legislation that would hinder the activities of the traffickers and pimps. As corruption and collaboration increase, the line between the state and the criminal networks starts to blur. This merging of criminal networks and government has occurred in many of the former Soviet republics, which are the major suppliers of women to the brothels of Europe. Reports from the Netherlands, Germany and Australia, indicate that legalized prostitution does not solve these problems, but leads to increased prostitution, trafficking and organized crime." (by Donna M. Hughes) [15]

As evident from the above quoted texts, many sensible people have been pointing out towards the debauchery of the feminist movement. Sexual objectification is the act of treating a person merely as an instrument of sexual pleasure, making them a 'sex object'. Objectification more broadly means treating a person as a commodity or an object, without regard to their personality or dignity. Feminists talk a lot against the 'objectification' of women but the actions of the debauched so-called liberal feminists are further promoting it. The people and groups who are working on feminist issues should have a clear understanding that liberty does not mean debauchery or nudity. Modesty is a good human virtue which differentiates human beings from animals. Mark Twain, renowned American humorist, writer, and lecturer, rightly said, "Clothes make the man. Naked people have little or no influence on society." [16]

Chapter 6

Islam And Women

"Whoever has a girl under his guardianship, and he neither bur-
ies her alive, nor treats her with contempt, nor give prefer-
ence to his sons over her, Allah will admit him to Paradise."
(Prophet Muhammad PBUH) [1]

WHAT IS ISLAM?

In Arabic the word 'Islam', means "submission", meaning submission to the will of God. Islam also means "peace", the peace one finds through submission to the will of God. The term 'Deen of Islam' can be defined as a collection of all those matters of obedience that Allah s.w.t (The God Almighty), through his Messengers, has made obligatory upon the people, by means of which His (God's) nearness and mercy is received. The Deen of Islam consists of the following teachings:

1. Basic matters and concepts that do not change with time e.g. basic faiths like the faith in one God, belief that God's commandments must be obeyed, basic moral teachings and ethics like speaking the truth. These concepts were conveyed to mankind without any alteration by all the Prophets sent by God throughout the human history.

2. However there were some other matters that changed with time depending upon the need of the time. For example certain commandments that were given to Hazrat Musa AS (Moses) changed during the prophethood of Hazrat Esa AS (Jesus). In the Holy Quran, Prophet Esa AS (Jesus) is reported to have said to the Children of Israel, "(I have come to you) to attest the Law which was before me and to make lawful to you part of what was (before) forbidden to you; I have come to you with a Sign from your Lord. So fear Allah and obey me." (Surah Al-i-Imran, Chapter 3, Ayat 50)

Present day adherents of Islam, called Muslims, believe Islam is the final message from God to humankind. It is a reconfirmation and perfection of the messages that God has revealed through earlier Prophets. According to Islamic Fiqah (jurisprudence) literature, the Deen of Islam deals with the following five types of matters:

1. DOGMAS (A system of belief): Belief in 'one God i.e Allah', 'Angels', 'Holy Books' like the Bible and the Holy Quran, 'Prophets' i.e the Messengers of God, and 'The Day of Judgment', to name a few.
2. ACTS OF WORSHIP: Salat (prayer), Zakat (charity), Saum (fasting), Hajj (pilgrimage), and Jihad (the Arabic word which means "to struggle or strive, to exert oneself" for a praiseworthy aim).
3. DEALINGS: Like financial matters, family matters, conflicts resolution and judicial matters, inheritance matters, and trust related matters.
4. PUNISHMENTS: Punishments for murder, expropriation of property, adultery/fornication, false allegation of adultery/fornication, apostasy, to name a few.
5. MANNERS: Ethics and morality, etiquettes and social virtues, government related matters, and other social matters [2].

On August 1941, the founder of Pakistan, Quaid-e-Azam Muhammad Ali Jinnah, went to Hyderabad Deccan (India) and gave an interview to the students of the Usmania University. His reply to the question, "What are the essential features of religion and a religious State?" was, "When I hear the word 'religion,' my mind thinks at once, according to the English language and the British usage, of private relation between man and God. But I know fully well that according to Islam, the word is not restricted to the English connotation. I am neither a Maulvi nor a Mulla, nor do I claim knowledge of theology. But I have studied in my own way, the Holy Quran and Islamic tenets. This magnificent Book is full of guidance respecting all human life, whether spiritual or economic, political or social, leaving no aspect untouched." [3]

World renowned Islamic scholar Mufti Muhammad Taqi Usmani further elaborates this concept, "He (God) has created man and appointed
him as His vicegerent on the earth to fulfill certain objectives through
obeying His commands. These commands are not restricted to some
modes of worship or so-called religious rituals. They, on the contrary,
cover a substantial area of almost every activity of life. These commands are neither so exhaustive that straiten the human activities within
a narrow circle, leaving no room for human intellect to play, nor they are
so little and ambiguous that they leave every sphere of life at the mercy
of human perception and desire. Far from these two extremes, Islam
has a balanced approach to govern the human life. On the one hand, it
has left a wide area of human activities to man's own rational judgment
where he can take decisions on the basis of his reason, assessment of
facts and expedience. On the other hand, Islam has subjected human
activities to a set of principles which have eternal application and cannot be violated on superficial grounds of expediency based on human
assessment. The fact behind this scheme is that human reason, despite
vast capabilities, cannot claim to have unlimited power to reach the
truth. There are numerous domains of the human life where 'reason'
is often confused with 'desires' and where unhealthy instincts, under
the disguise of rational arguments misguide humanity to wrong and
destructive decisions. All those theories of the past which are held today
to be fallacious, claimed, in their respective times, to be 'rational' but it
were after centuries that their fallacy was discovered and their absur-
dity was universally proved. It is thus evident that the sphere of work
delegated to human 'reason' by its Creator is not unlimited. There are
areas in which human reason cannot give proper guidance or, at least,
is susceptible to errors. It is these areas in which Allah Almighty, the
Creator of the universe, has provided guidance through His revelations
sent down to His Prophets." [4]

Islam and social justice:

In order to avoid exploitation and injustice in a society, there is a need
for establishing a system based on social justice. Historically, mankind is

trying to find a 'point of justice' between the following three basic but very complex issues:

1. Man and Woman: Imperative for the establishment of a just social system.
2. Capital and Labour: Imperative for the establishment of a just economic system.
3. Individual and State: Imperative for the establishment of a just political system.

For us finding out an exact point of justice for these complex matters is practically impossible due to human limitations. Historically, mankind has taken various positions on these issues.

Every system is epitomized by a slogan. For example, the slogan for Capitalism is 'Liberty / Freedom'. Liberty is a good virtue to target but the problem is that when we try to give perfect liberty to individuals then we tend to lose the other good virtue of 'Equality'. Following quotes of some notables regarding Liberty and Capitalism acknowledges this fact.

"Advocates of Capitalism are very apt to appeal to the sacred principles of liberty, which are embodied in one maxim: The fortunate must not be restrained in the exercise of tyranny over the unfortunate." (Bertrand Russell, English Logician and Philosopher 1872-1970)

"When liberty comes with hands dabbled in blood it is hard to shake hands with her." (Oscar Wilde, French Philosopher and Writer, 1694-1778)

"The forces in a Capitalist society, if left unchecked, tend to make the rich richer and the poor poorer." (Jawaharlal Nehru, Indian Prime Minister. 1889-1964) [5]

This is the result of absolute and unconditional freedom. Even today the situation is dismal in the Capitalist countries. American filmmaker, author, social critic and activist Michael Moore (of 'Fahrenheit 9/11' fame) in his movie 'Capitalism: A Love Story', reveals many problems being faced by the citizens of a Capitalist society especially the problem of the very unbalanced distribution of wealth. The movie trailer says, "'Capitalism: A Love Story' comes home to the issue he's (Michael Moore) been examining throughout his career: The disastrous impact of corporate dominance on the everyday life of Americans. But this time the culprit is much bigger than General Motors, and the crime scene is far wider than Flint, Michigan." [6]

After observing the evils of pure Capitalist systems and as a reaction to it, Communist movements started in many parts of the world that promulgated the concept of 'Equality.' Again, equality is a good virtue to target but the problem is that we tend to lose the other good virtue of 'Liberty' when we try to make everyone forcefully equal. Following quotes of some luminaries regarding Communism acknowledges this fact.

"It is not alone that property, in all its forms, is struck at, but that liberty, in all its forms, is challenged by the fundamental conceptions of Socialism" (Winston Churchill, British Orator, Author and Prime Minister during World War II, 1874-1965)

"Communism means barbarism" (James Russell, American Poet, Critic, Essayist, Editor and Diplomat, 1819-1891) [7]

This emphatic statement by James Russell can be examined in the light of somewhat disturbing historical fact. Michael Hart, an astrophysicist and a history writer, while mentioning the history of Communism in his famous book 'The 100' writes, "Stalin's ruthless use of the secret police, and his program of arbitrary arrests and executions, and long terms in prison or labour camps for anyone even slightly critical to his rule, succeeded in cowing the population into submission. By the end of 1930s he had created perhaps the most totalitarian dictatorship of modern times, a government structure which intruded into every aspect of life and under which there were no civil liberties." [8]

Islam emphasizes 'Justice.' According to the Holy Quran, "Lo! Allah enjoineth justice and kindness, and giving to kinsfolk, and forbiddeth lewdness and abomination and wickedness. He exhorteth you in order that ye may take heed." (Surah An-Nahl, Chapter 16, Verse 90). "You who believe! Be upholders of justice, bearing witness for Allah alone, even against yourselves or your parents and relatives. Whether they are rich or poor, Allah is well able to look after them. Do not follow your own desires and deviate from the truth. If you twist or turn away, Allah is aware of what you do." (Surah Nisa', Chapter 4, Verse 135)

Islam even does justice between values of 'Liberty' and 'Equality'. Islam believes in liberty but with certain checks and balances so that the other good value of equality is not lost in the process. The concept of freedom in a Capitalistic system means absolute and unrestricted freedom based on the doctrine of Laissez Faire. In the Islamic system, there is conditional freedom that is subject to two major qualifications: 1) The dictates of ethics, and 2) The interest of the community at large. For example, contrary to the practice of some Western nations, in an Islamic system, one cannot draw and publish the cartoons of the Holy Prophets in the name of 'Freedom of Expression'. This deplorable act is absolutely against the fundamental human ethics and therefore not allowed in Islam.

Following are quotes of two eminent non-Muslim personalities regarding Islam.

"Sense of justice is one of the most wonderful ideals of Islam, because as I read in the Quran I find those dynamic principles of life, not mystic but practical ethics for the daily conduct of life suited to the whole world." (Sarojini Naidu, a child prodigy, freedom fighter and a poet, also called Nightingale of India) [9]

"I hope the time is not far off when I shall be able to unite all the wise and educated men of all the countries and establish a uniform regime based on the principles of Qur'an which alone are true and which alone can lead men to happiness." (Napolean Bonaparte, a celebrated French General and Emperor) [10]

The readers who are interested in knowing more about Islam can consult my book ISLAM: A SUPERIOR SYSTEM OF LIFE [11], which will give you a comprehensive view of Islam at a single place.

ISLAM A SAVIOUR OF WOMEN

The Greek civilization is considered the most glorious of all ancient civilizations. Under this very 'glorious' system, women were deprived of all rights and were looked down upon. According to ancient Greek mythology, the very first woman was created out of earth by Hephaestus at the request of Zeus, the king of the gods, and sent down into the world with a box containing all kinds of misery and evil. It was the intention of Zeus to punish Prometheus who had stolen fire from the heaven and bestowed it upon the mortals. The story goes that from the moment the box was opened, the world has been plagued with wickedness and sorrow. This woman was given the name of Pandora, a Greek word which originally meant 'all-giving', but which came to be synonymous with 'giver of all evils'. The box that she brought with her is called the Pandora Box. This is only one of the examples of perception about the women that were prevalent during the course of history. Following are some more glimpses of the pre-Islamic era:

- Women were degraded and were denied all rights under the Babylonian law. If a man murdered a woman, instead of him being punished, his wife was put to death.
- In old Persia, women were estates and therefore could be sold as you can sell your farm.
- In the Roman Empire, Roman Law gave no rights to women. Woman could not be the owner of any kind of property. When Roman Civilization was at the zenith of its 'glory', a man even

had the right to take the life of his wife. Prostitution and nudity were common amongst the Romans.

- The Egyptian considered women as evil and a sign of a devil.
- In the old Indian civilization, woman had no permanent rights. Her life ends with the death of her husband. According to Hindu religion, a woman is burnt alive with the dead body of her husband. This practice is called 'Sati'.
- In Christianity, a woman was considered as a source of evil. According to some scholars, the word 'Evil' is derived from the word 'Eve'. There was a great symposium held in France in 586 AD wherein it was settled through a proposition that woman has been created only for the service of male, and as a permanent creature she has no rights and role.
- In pre-Islamic Arabia, the Arabs looked down upon women and very often when a female child was born, she was buried alive.

This was the global social environment at the time of the advent of Islam which brought with it revolutionary teachings regarding various matters including that of the status of women.. Following guidance was revealed by Allah s.w.t in the Holy Quran regarding the relationship of husband and wife: "…..they are your garments. And ye are their garments….." (Surah Al-Baqara, Chapter 2, Verse 187)

If we put all that whatever is written and said till now regarding women rights in one pan of a scale and put this verse of the Holy Quran on the other pan of the scale, then the Quranic verse would prove to be heavier. The Islamic teachings completely changed the status of women in a society. Many rights that Islam granted to women were not enjoyed until later centuries by women living in other parts of the world. Ms. Yvonne Ridley is a former non-Muslim British journalist, and war correspondent. She writes in her article, "A careful reading of the Quran shows that just about everything that Western feminists fought for in the 1970s, was available to Muslim women 1400 years ago." [12] The following discussion mentions some of such rights that were granted by Islam to women.

WOMEN RIGHTS AS GRANTED BY ISLAM

Islam has bestowed upon women innumerable rights, around fourteen centuries back, when contemporary civilizations were still considering whether women could be regarded as a human being or not. Following are some of the basic rights that Islam grants to women. Many of these rights were not enjoyed by Western Women till many centuries later. Ms. Annie Besant was a British theosophist, women's rights activist, writer & orator. She writes, "I often think that woman is more free in Islam than in Christianity... In Al-Quran the law about women is more just & liberal. It is only in the last twenty years that Christian England has recognized the right of woman to property, while Islam has allowed this right from all times,...It is a slander to say that Islam preaches that women have no souls." [13]

Right to an education:

Prophet Muhammad (PBUH) said, "Seeking knowledge is obligatory for every Muslim". (Ibn Maja) Please note that this saying of the Holy Prophet (PBUH) does not differentiate between men and women for seeking knowledge.

Islamic scholars inform that the obligatory knowledge, as mentioned in this Hadith, is the basic religious knowledge that is required by every person to lead a complete life in accordance with Islamic teachings. Acquiring at least this much knowledge is obligatory on each and every Muslim, whether men or women, depending on their respective needs. In other knowledge areas as well, Islam finds nothing wrong with females acquiring education. However the education system should be designed keeping in view the Islamic norms and guidance for the society. For example, Islam does not allow the free mixing of the sexes. Also the education system for girls should also include the topics of their needs and necessities.

Nur ud-Deen Zangi was a very famous Muslim ruler. He ruled Syria from 541 AH to 569 AH (1146 - 1174 CE). He was a just and righteous leader and was well-loved by those under him. Dr. Ali Muhammad As-Sallabi, in his 'Ad-Dawla az Zankiyya', a historical account of the Zangi era wrote about women's education in the rule of Nur ud-Deen Zangi. The following is a translation of the chapter on women's education:

"The devotion of Muslim women to Islamic studies reached high levels. Their purpose was to gain knowledge of the correct teachings of the religion and thereby bring them into practice. The subject that received the most regard was the study of Hadith, in which many women attained high qualification. They competed with great Hadith scholars and memorizers of Hadith therein and became profound examples of trust-worthiness and uprightness.

Many biographical accounts allude to the substantial intellectual activities of women in this era. Sources have mentioned names of numerous female Qaris, hadith scholars, fiqh scholars, writers, grammarians, as well as scholars of other fundamental sciences. Many of these women would travel from region to region with their maharim (close male relative like husband, father, brother, son, etc) to seek knowledge from great scholars and Muhaddithin and they received ijazas (certificates) from them. A testimony to the undertakings of women in this field is the fact that the biographers of Ibn Asakir (d. 571 AH / 1176) agree that more than eighty of his teachers were women. This demonstrates the large numbers of women who were busy in this field, such that a single scholar from the scholars of that era studied from more than eighty women. This is in addition to the large number of women whose biographies he has included in his book. (Ibn Asakir collected biographical accounts of 196 women scholars in his tareekh).

It becomes apparent from what Ibn Asakir alludes to in his Tarikh al-Kabir that the home was the first school for these women. The women who received much acclaim for their knowledge were the ones who grew up in the houses of scholars and studied from their fathers or other knowledgeable relatives. These women would also benefit from the various classes that would take place in their homes, as they would listen to what was being discussed. This is what is listed as "Teaching in the homes of the scholars" in historical accounts. Thus, when Ibn Asakir wrote about his wife, Aisha bint Ali (d. 564 AH / 1168), he mentioned that she studied Hadith from Fatima bint Ali Al-Asfraini, known as the Young Scholar, who in turn had studied with her father Abul Farj.

Similarly, the doors of the Masjid (mosque) would be open for women who wanted to study. These women would frequent the study circles that took place in the Masjid. These study circles had a specific space appropriated for them, a space which was totally separated from that of men which eliminated the possibility of mingling of the genders.

Women did not just take part in studying, but rather they played a role in spreading and teaching knowledge as well. Although they did not have teaching positions in specialized schools in the manner we see now, they did have other avenues of teaching. Ibn Asakir indicates this as he writes about his wife's teacher Fatima bint Ali Al-Asfraini that she used to give sermons to women in the Masjid.

One of the most notable women in the field of teaching was the alima Fatima al-Faqiha. She taught in Halab and authored many works of fiqh and hadith. Further, Nur-ud Din, the ruler of the era, would consult with her in his affairs and ask her for fatawa in fiqhi issues. He supported her and helped her in her educational pursuits.

An event that transpired between Fatima al-Faqiha and Nur-ud Din highlights the commitment of the Muslim women to the Islamic requirement of Hijab (veil) and how the female scholars would only communicate with men through a woman assigned to act as a middle-person. The event, as Al-Qurashi writes, is that 'Ala ad-Deen al-Kasani, the husband of the scholar Fatima al-Faqiha, decided to move from Halab to his own country at the request of his wife. Nur ud Deen summoned Imam Ala ad-Deen and requested him to stay in Halab. Imam Ala ud-Deen explained to him the reason for his move and told him that he could not oppose his wife's wish who was also the daughter of his Shaikh. Nur ud-Deen then sent a servant to Fatima to speak to her on his behalf. When the servant arrived at her house, she did not allow him to enter. Then she sent someone to her husband (who was with the king at that time) with the message, "With your experience and knowledge of fiqh, don't you know that it's not permissible for this servant to see me? What's the difference between him and other men?" The servant returned and recounted what had taken place to her husband in the presence of the ruler. They then sent a woman to her with the king's request. Fatima then accepted the request and stayed in Halab until she passed away.

Her husband al-Kasani passed away after her in 587 AH / 1191 and was buried next to her in Halab." [14]

Right to own wealth and property:

Women have a right to own, sell, purchase, rent, or donate property and assets. They have a right to own and control their holdings. A woman has the right to keep her property or wealth, whether earned or inherited, and spend it as she may please.

Right to inheritance:

Islam gives women right to inheritance. Islam gives detailed instructions about how to distribute the inheritance among legal heirs including women. According to the Holy Quran, "For men there is a share in what the parents and the nearest of kin have left. And for women there is a share in what the parents and the nearest of kin have left, be it small or large - a determined share." (Surah An-Nisa, Chapter 4, Ayat 7)

Right to choose a husband:

The guardian of the girl, whether her father, brother or uncle, plays an important role in her marriage such as finding a suitable match for her. But under no circumstances does this allow him to force his choice on her against her wishes. She is free to accept or reject his choice, or make her own choice. According to a famous book on Islamic jurisprudence, "Adult woman is free whether she marries or not. And to marry whom she wishes to marry and not to marry with whom she does not wish to marry. 'Wali' (guardian) can neither stop her from marrying nor forcefully marry her without her will and nor forcefully marry her somewhere as per his or her wish." [15]

Right of being taken care of:

A very big favor of Islam on women is that the burden of earning the livelihood is not placed on her shoulders. At any stage in her life, she is never asked to labour or earn for herself or for her family members. It is the duty of man, her father, her husband, her brother or her son to feed her and look after all her financial necessities. This is a woman's legal right which she can claim in a court against her nearest relative. And if she has no relative, she can claim her livelihood from the government of an Islamic State, in any court of justice.

Ms. Annie Besant while mentioning the condition of Western women writes in her book, "...and do not look at what lies behind it in the West – the frightful degradation of women who are thrown into the streets when their first protectors, weary of them, no longer give them any assistance." [16]

Right to earn money:

Although as per Islamic teachings this is not her duty but a woman is allowed to earn. There are occasions due to which a woman has to go out from her home to earn the livelihood, for example, there is no one to fulfill her financial needs. Whenever a female leaves her home, she must adhere to the Islamic code of living. It is also the responsibility of the Muslim community to organize work for women, so that she can do so as per the Muslim cultural atmosphere, where her rights are respected. A detailed discussion on this topic is comming in the next chapter.

Freedom of expression:

Caliph Umer (RAA) was once standing on the pulpit, reprimanding the people and ordering them not to set excessive amounts of dower at the time of marriage. A woman got up and shouted, "Umar! You have no right to intervene in a matter which Allah the All-Mighty has already decreed in the Quran:" If you want to take a wife in place of the one (you have), and you have given her plenty of wealth, then do not take any of it back. Would you take it through imputation and open sin? (Surah An-Nisa, Chapter 4, verse 20) After being reminded of this Verse, Hazrat Umer (RAA) withdrew his order, saying, "I am in the wrong and she is correct."

Here I would also like to introduce Caliph Umer (RAA), in front of whom this woman expressed her apposing views. Just to have an idea about the power and influence of Caliph Umer (RAA), I want to mention that the famous history writer Michael Hart has included the name of Caliph Umer (RAA) in his famous book 'The 100' in which he has discussed the top 100 most influential personalities in the history of human kind. In his chapter about Caliph Umer (RAA) he writes, "It may occasion some surprise that 'Umar' – a figure virtually unknown to the West – has been ranked higher that such famous men as Charlemagne and Julius Caesar. However, the conquests made by the Arabs under 'Umar', taking into account both their size and their duration, are substantially more important than those of either Caesar or Charlemagne." [17]

Giving input in political / policy matters:

Following are some examples of the political and administrative matters where women advice was taken by Prophet Muhammad (PBUH) or his pious companions:

- On the famous occasion of 'Truce of Hudaibiya', Prophet Muhammad (PBUH) discussed a problem with his wife Hazrat Um Salma (RAA). She gave a very valuable piece of advice to the Prophet (PBUH). Prophet Muhammad (PBUH) acted as per her advice and the problem eventually resolved very well.
- Caliph Umer (RAA) consulted and took the advice of his daughter (Hazrat Hafsa RAA) while making the law limiting the period a Mujahid (a person on a Holy war) can spend in Jihad (Holy war) away from his wife, to four months.
- While consulting people for making the future caliph (after Hazrat Umer RAA), it is written that Hazrat Abdur Rehman bin Aaof (RAA) even went to consult the women of Hijab (veiled women at their homes) to take their input.

It is evident from these three quoted examples that a Muslim woman has a right to give her input in political and policy matters.

I am reproducing here a short article by a Muslim woman, Syeda Akefah Hashmi, on the topic of women's education in Islam. This article not only discusses education but clarifies many other matters with respect to women rights. Following is her article:

Women's Education in Islam [18]

Like all matters of the universe, the existence of man and woman in this world is for balance of the cosmos, to keep the scales at a predetermined state and preventing them from tipping either way. Chinese philosophy proclaims this as Ying and Yang, where both are required to maintain the natural harmony of nature. This is what was decided for those before us and those after us.

Equality does not mean being the exact copies of each other or handling the other's responsibilities. These have been sorted out while the stars were still young. Being equal means intermingling and sharing in such a way that the burden is divided over all shoulders, where neither feels encumbered in their own self.

The prevailing attitude in the current society has made it a handicapped one. It may limp along with one leg but it would never achieve in running to the finish line or perhaps even reaching the first stop. Islam does not need females to be spineless or meek; they weren't made to be suppressed under unjust traditions. Keeping within the prescribed limits, females are allowed to achieve their full potential, which is more than just raising kids.

Family is the cornerstone of a person's life and mainly the females keep it together. But no way does this mean that a female cannot have independent thoughts or talents which she can utilize. She has opinions of her own and wise ideas that can benefit those who ask for them. Under the flag of Caliph Umar Farooq (RAU), females were given seats in the parliament (majlis-e shuura) given their opinions are invaluable advice. For some things can only be understood by the female mind and as Allah (SWT) has created it for use, it was put to test and came clear all the time.

The Holy Prophet (SAW) said: "Acquisition of knowledge is binding on all Muslims (both men and women without any discrimination)" (Sunan Ibn Maja).

Islam finds nothing wrong with females acquiring education and in fact even encourages it. Those who have embraced the true meaning of Islam have minds as bright and open as pane-less windows facing the sun. Khawlah (RAM) was a Muslim woman whose husband Aws (RAU) pronounced this statement at a moment of anger: "You are to me as the back of my mother". This was held by pagan Arabs to be a statement of divorce which freed the husband from any conjugal responsibility but did not leave the wife free to leave the husband's home or to marry another man. Having heard these words from her husband, Khawlah (RAM) was in a miserable situation. She went straight to the Prophet of Islam (SAW) to plead her case. The Prophet (SAW) was of the opinion that she should be patient since there seemed to be no way out. Khawla (RAM) kept arguing with the Prophet (SAW) in an attempt to save her suspended marriage. Shortly, the Quran intervened; Khawla's (RAM) plea was accepted. The divine verdict abolished this iniquitous custom: "Allah has heard and accepted the statement of the woman who pleads with you (the Prophet) concerning her husband and carries her complaint to Allah, and Allah hears the arguments between both of you for Allah hears and sees all things...." (Quran 58:1).

This incident shows that females could dialogue with the Prophet (SAW), stating their thinking and asking for their rights. She does not have to blindly accept the dominant male person in her life as being the sole source of just rules, Allah (SWT) has granted the double X chromosome carriers brains as well and the ability to utilize them. And since nothing was created without a purpose, keeping in mind the regulations of Islam and one's own limitations, females can reach the top of every ladder while still maintaining her dignity and beliefs.

The Holy Prophet (SAW) said at another place: "Allah Almighty makes the path to paradise easier for him who walks on it for getting knowledge." (Sahih Muslim)

Therefore, it is clear that the gaining of knowledge is encouraged regardless of gender and is in fact, said to be rewarded with each procurement. Islam has set clear guidelines for females and knowledge is coveted everywhere and is not forbidden to those who observe the veil as shown by examples in the Holy Prophet's (SAW) life.

Abu Sa'id Khudri (RAU) reports that women said to the Holy Prophet (SAW): 'Men have gone ahead of us (in terms of acquisition of knowledge). Therefore, appoint a special day for our benefit as well.' The Holy Prophet (SAW) fixed one day for them. He (SAW) would meet them on that day, advise them and educate them about commandments of Allah Almighty. (Sahih Bukhari)

This clears another misunderstanding in the minds of people as to males could not tutor female students. Under the observance of veil and proper Islamic guidelines, females are not to be deprived of their chance at better religious education just for lack of a feminine tutor as can be obvious from the fact that our own Holy Prophet (SAW) taught those who wanted to expand their horizons.

Sayyida 'A'isha Siddiqa (RAM), mother of the faithful, was a hadith-narrator, scholar, intellectual and jurist of great standing. She is believed to have reported 2,210 traditions. Abu Hurayra (RAU), 'Abdullah ibn 'Amr (RAU) and Anas ibn Malik (RAU) were the only ones from amongst male hadith narrators who had narrated more traditions than she did. This shows that women could not only teach women but also men after fulfilling certain preconditions. (Article by Syeda Akefah Hashmi)

JUSTICE BETWEEN MEN AND WOMEN

The following text analyzes the status of men and women from three different angles. These are:

1. As human beings
2. Administrative point of view
3. Honor, respect, and good treatment

As human beings:

Till the fifteenth century, the responsible people of the Church were seriously thinking about the nature of women. It was being discussed whether they have souls on which the salvation in the hereafter depends. Most people shared the view that a woman does not have such a soul.

Hazrat Maryam AS (Mary) was considered as an exception. As mentioned earlier in this book, in France, there was a great symposium in 586 AD wherein it was settled through a proposition that women have been created only for the service of male, and as a permanent creature she has got no rights and role.

As per Islam no one is of superior or inferior caste just based on their gender. It is possible that a husband is the worst human being like Pharaoh and his wife a superior human being i.e Hazrat Aseya (AS). In the Holy Quran both men and women are referred to as garments for each other. Both have separate identities. They have a system of mutual rights and obligations. Prophet Muhammad (PBUH) said, "O People, it is true that you have certain rights over your women, but they also have rights over you." (Last Sermon)

Both will receive reward from Allah for the good deeds they have done. According to the Holy Quran, "Surely, Muslim men and Muslim women, believing men and believing women, devout men and devout women, truthful men and truthful women, patient men and patient women, humble men and humble women, and the men who give Sadaqah (charity) and the women who give Sadaqah, and the men who fast and the women who fast, and the men who guard their private parts (against evil acts) and the women who guard (theirs), and the men who remember Allah much and the women who remember (Him) – for them, Allah has prepared forgiveness and a great reward. (Surah Al-Ahzab, Chapter 33, verse 35)

Muslim history is full of great women heroes like Hazrat Khadeeja (RAA), Hazrat Ayesha (RAA), Hazrat Fatima (RAA), Hazrat Rabia Basri, and Hazrat Zubaida. Take the example of Hazrat Ayesha (RAA), an extremely intelligent woman who was one of the wives of Prophet Muhammad (PBUH). Being much younger than he was, she survived him by about fifty years, and, with her excellent, almost photographic memory, she was able to continue to communicate in great detail everything that she had learned from him during their very close companionship. Therefore for about half a century she was able to fulfill a highly informative role. She taught religion to around 200 students. Many other Sahaba (companions of the Prophet PBUH) and Tabiyeen (companions of Sahaba) acquired religious knowledge from her.

Administrative point of view:

Family is the basic organizational unit of a society. The smooth functioning of the family also requires a single CEO (Chief Executive Officer) just like any commercial organization that cannot work effectively and efficiently with more than one CEO. Therefore, whenever a man and a woman, who are equal human beings, enter into the relationship of husband and wife, the man is given the administrative post of the head of the family. In this particular respect therefore his rank is higher than that of woman. As a head of a family he is made responsible for fulfilling the needs of the whole family. In a commercial organization a person of higher responsibility is also given a higher authority in certain matters thus enabling him or her to cope with the higher level of responsibility. The same is true for a family where a man, as the head of the family, is given more authority in certain matters.

Allah s.w.t says in the Holy Quran: "Men are in-charge of women, because Allah has given the one more than the other and because they spend of their property (for the support of women)..." (Surah An-Nisa, Chapter 4, verse 34)

When we read this verse of the Holy Quran in Arabic then we see that Allah s.w.t has not used the word 'ameer' (leader) or 'hakim' (ruler) or 'malik' (king), instead Allah s.w.t has used the word 'qaw'wam' which means someone who is responsible for a certain job. The responsibility here is that the man will set the overall guidelines for living life and then these guidelines will have to be followed. 'Qaw'wam' does not mean that the man is the master and his wife is his maid or servant. The relationship is that of leader and the subordinate. And in Islam the concept of the ruler is, 'The leader of a nation is the true servant of the nation'. The following sayings of Prophet Muhammad (PBUH) will make this concept about leaders crystal clear:

"If anyone who has been given responsibility regarding any matter concerning Muslims, and he ignores the needs of the Muslims neglecting their distress and withdraws himself, Allah in the Hereafter will ignore his needs and distress and withdraw from him." (Abu Dawood, Tirmizi)

"Allah will forbid Paradise to the one whom Allah gives supervision of the people and he dies neglecting his obligations." (Sahih Bukhari, Sahih Muslim)

Today when we think of a leader such kings and heads of states come into our mind who do not even consider it necessary to talk to the people. However in Islam the concept of a leader is that of a servant, that is the one who serves others. No doubt that a leader has authority to give orders but his orders will be for serving his people, for their welfare and their comfort.

As already discussed, men are 'qaw'wam' over women but the relationship between them should also be like that of friends. Allah says in the Holy Quran, "And it is among His signs that He has created for you wives from among yourselves, so that you may find tranquility in them, and He has created love and kindness between you. Surely in this there are signs for a people who reflect." (Surah Ar-Rome, Chapter 30, verse 21)

In this Ayat of the Holy Quran, Allah s.w.t is mentioning the relationship of love and kindness among the husband and the wife as one of His signs. This is what is actually required by Islam. For running the family affairs, man is indeed in-charge but the husband and wife are also good friends and not like a master and his maid. They are like two friends traveling together in a journey and one appointing the other as the leader. The husband has the authority to take decisions necessary for their journey but this does not mean that he treats his wife like a servant or a slave. This friendship between husband and wife, however, is about some requirements and certain manners. These include bearing with the whims and airs of the wife which does not change the role of the one in charge. Being in-charge does not mean that the family starts fearing the head of the family so much that they cannot even talk to him. The Prophet (PBUH) said, "The worst of the people is he who makes life hard for his family members." (Kanz-ul-Aamal)

After marriage a man finds in a form of a wife a very good friend, partner, advisor, and supporter. A good wife can really be a blessing for a husband and a good husband a blessing for a wife. Muslims are advised to run their matters with mutual consultation. Prophet Muhammad (PBUH) himself consulted his companions and his wives in many important matters. On the famous occasion of 'Truce of Hudaibiya', Prophet Muhammad (PBUH) discussed a problem with his wife, Hazrat Um Salma (RAA). She gave a very valuable piece of advice to the Prophet (PBUH). Prophet Muhammad (PBUH) acted as per her advice and the problem eventually resolved very well.

In his speech at Jinnah Islamia College for Girls, the founder of Pakistan Quaid-e-Azam Muhammad Ali Jinnah said, "I am glad to see that not only Muslim men but Muslim women and children also have understood the Pakistan scheme. No nation can make any progress without the co-operation of its women. If Muslim women support their men, as they did in the days of the Prophet of Islam (PBUH), we should soon realize our goal." [19]

There are many examples of bad head of families throughout the world. In USA intimate partner violence made up 20% of all nonfatal violent crime experienced by women in 2001. In 2000, 1,247 women and 440 men were killed by an intimate partner. In recent years, an intimate partner killed approximately 33% of female murder victims and 4% of male murder victims. [20] Numerous television channels have shown reports discussing the problem of domestic violence against women.

In some cases even baseball bats were used to batter wives. A few years back BBC television news reported that on an average 3000 women are killed per year in the USA by their husbands and boyfriends. That's an unbelievable figure!

If a Muslim man really wants to practice Islam, then he must treat his wife and family well. Despite these teachings there are numerous bad examples in the modern Muslim world as well. The people who are not treating their wives and other family members well are definitely not practicing Islam. They are far away from Islam. They do not represent Islam.

This is not the case that the status of women was high in the world and Islam has degraded them by declaring the men as heads of the family. Islam actually is mentioning a natural universal fact without any hypocrisy, the hypocrisy that many other people are displaying. In almost all cultures, Muslim or non-Muslim, a husband is generally considered the head of the family. Consider the following examples:

According to the Bible, "Wives should be submissive to their husbands, that the word of God may not be discredited." (Titus 2:5.)

According to a famous Chinese proverb, "Man is the head of the family, woman the neck that turns the head."

USSR was a society where equality of men and women was very much emphasized and promoted on the state level. But the reality on ground was contrary. Patrice C. McMahon mentions about the relationship of men and women in the Communist Russian society as, "…relationships between men and women were characterized by the latter's strict subordination and obedience to men rather than by equality and partnership." [22] Please note that Prophet Muhammad PBUH in one of his sayings has declared women as partners to men. He (PBUH) said, "Do treat your women well and be kind to them for they are your partners and committed helpers." (Last Sermon)

Mr. Philip Cohen in his article 'America is still a Patriarchy' writes, "In my own area of research things are messier, because families and workplaces differ so much and power is usually jointly held. But I'm confident in describing American families as mostly patriarchal. Maybe the most basic indicator is the apparently quaint custom of wives assuming their husbands' names. This hasn't generated much feminist controversy lately. But to an anthropologist from another planet, this patrilineality would be a major signal that American families are male-dominated. Among U.S.- born married women, only 6 percent had a surname that differed from their husband's in 2004 (it was not until the 1970s that married women could even function legally using their "maiden" names). Among the youngest women the rate is higher, so there is a clear pattern of change—but no end to the tradition in sight. Of course, the proportion of people getting married has fallen, and the number of children born to non-married parents has risen. Single parenthood—and the fact that this usually means single motherhood—reflects both women's growing independence and the burdens of care that fall on them (another piece of the patriarchal puzzle). This is one of many very important changes. But they don't add up to a non-patriarchal society." [23]

Please note that although this phenomenon is quite common in some Muslim countries as well, this is not an Islamic practice that a wife should use the name of her husband in her name. Case in point: my wife did not change her name after we got married. We depend on each other being a husband and a wife, but we both have independent identities, individual personalities and differing opinions on various matters. We both are Muslims.

<u>Is it only the 'Social Construct' to blame?</u> Feminists, who insist on strict equality of men and women in every respect, claim that the global domination of men is due to the 'social construct' of the societies. According to them somehow men's dominance and leadership was globally accepted in the human societies throughout the world otherwise there is no scientific or any other valid reason for it. Professor Steven Golberg is a

native of New York City and was president of the sociology department at City College of New York from 1988 till his retirement. He in his book 'The Inevitability of Patriarchy' writes, "It is a rough old world for women, as the feminists never cease to remind us. They blame centuries of social conditioning - a kind of conspiracy whereby men all over the world somehow contrive to keep women in a subordinate role. A much simpler, and more probable explanation is that universal male dominance stems not from social oppression but fundamental differences between the sexes." [24]

Scientifically speaking, there are many differences between men and women which are responsible for the behavior of the two sexes in a society. Allan Mazur of Syracuse University and Alan Booth of the Sociology Department at Pennsylvania State University, in their scientific article 'Testosterone and Dominance in Men' explain, "In men, high levels of endogenous testosterone (T) seem to encourage behavior apparently intended to dominate -- to enhance one's status over -- other people. Sometimes dominant behavior is aggressive, its apparent intent being to inflict harm on another person, but often dominance is expressed non-aggressively. Sometimes dominant behavior takes the form of antisocial behavior, including rebellion against authority and law breaking. Measurement of T at a single point in time, presumably indicative of a man's basal T level, predicts many of these dominant or antisocial behaviors. T not only affects behavior but also responds to it." [25]

These testosterone levels are set away from the society while the baby is still in the mother's womb. According to the scientific article 'Programmed by Fetal Testosterone, Study Finds' published in LiveScience, "Testosterone levels during early fetal development might program certain behaviors later in life, according to a new study that found high levels of the sex hormone in the womb might boost boys' impulsivity later on. Researchers studied a group of boys ages 8 to 11 whose fetal testosterone had been measured from amniotic fluid when their mothers were 13-20 weeks pregnant. Sex hormone levels, which increase during adolescence, are also heightened during critical periods of fetal brain development." [26]

As mentioned in chapter 4 of this book, Ms. Heidi in her article 'Difference between male and female structures' explains, "No one can really tell whether these gender differences are caused by nature or environment-learned, but the fact is that some amount of sex differentiation takes place immediately as the male or female begins to develop within the womb. Some differences (such as reproductive organs) are congenital, while others obviously environmental (such as given names). Contrary to the beliefs of feminists or bisexuals, several studies have proven that there are expressed differences between males and females programmed within the DNA from the moment of conception." [27]

Even physically women are weaker than men in many ways. I will again quote here some of the differences as mentioned by Ms. Heidi in her article:

- An average man is taller and heavier than an average woman.
- Men are over 30% stronger than women, especially in the upper body. Although many feminists cannot face this fact, females simply do not have the strength or endurance necessary to be, for example, effective combat soldiers.
- Men have larger hearts and lungs, and their higher levels of testosterone cause them to produce greater amounts of red blood cells
- Differences in intake and delivery of oxygen translate into some aspects of performance: when a man is jogging at about 50% of his capacity, a woman will need to work at over 70% of her capacity to keep up with him.
- Female fertility decreases after age 35, ending with menopause, but men are capable of making children even when very old.
- Men's skin has more collagen and sebum, which makes it thicker and oilier than women's skin

- An average male brain has approximately 4% more cells and 100 grams more brain tissue than an average female brain. This is not connected with intelligence! Research points to no overall difference in intelligence between males and females. However, both sexes have similar brain weight to body weight ratios.

Women's physical weakness as compared with men in no way implies their inferiority. The eyes are the most delicate parts of the body, while the nails by comparison are extremely hard. This does not mean that the nails are superior to eyes. If a tiger is physically stronger than a human being then this does not mean that by virtue of his physical strength, the tiger is superior to human beings.

As evident from the above discussion, the universal male dominance is not just due to 'Social Construct', as asserted by some Feminists. That is why, despite full efforts at the state level in some societies, things remained unchanged. Russian Scientist Anton Nemilov, explains the Russian experience in his book, "Very few people will agree if it is said today that women should be given limited rights in the social setup. We, too, are wholly against such a suggestion. However, we should not deceive ourselves in thinking that establishing equality between men and women in practical life is a simple matter. Nowhere have more attempts been made than in the USSR to establish this equality. Nowhere in the world have such unbiased and generous laws been made than in the USSR, yet it is a fact that the position of woman in a family has hardly changed for the better." [28]

The tenets of Islam are based wholly on nature. This is because Islam is the religion of nature. Islamic teachings require us to follow our own instinctive human requirements expressed in legal terms. Islam does not deny the natural instincts but channelizes and disciplines them to minimize the chances of any unwanted behavior. For example there is an urge in human beings to copulate. Islam, therefore, promotes legal marriage but disapproves/condemns and even punishes adultery, fortification, incest, and homosexuality. Celibacy is not considered as an act of piety in Islam as it is against human nature.

The teachings of Islam with respect to women are no exception. Modern psychological, biological and anatomical research proves women to be more passive than men. This is the way their Maker (Allah s.w.t) has made them. This scheme is full of wisdom. The nature of their woman-hood, the special part they have to play in society, demands that they should be just as they have been made – that is, relatively delicate as compared to men. And this is part of their beauty.

The leadership role of a man in the family, which is close to his nature, can also result in some unwanted behavior. Men can show aggressive behavior towards women. As I said, Islam does not deny the natural instincts but channelizes and disciplines them to mini-mize the chances of any unwanted behavior. Similarly, Islam takes countermeasures against the potential aggressive behavior of men towards the women. Therefore Islamic teachings very much empha-size on the good treatment of women. Thus in this respect, the women have been given priority over men as evident from the fol-lowing discussion.

Honor / respect / good treatment:

Now we will analyze in detail what Islam has to teach the husbands, brothers, and sons, regarding the honor and respect of women. This is actually the area where Islam has given priority to women over men. A woman is a wife, a mother, a sister, or a daughter. I will analyze these four roles one by one, starting with the role of mother.

A mother is three times more 'eligible' for good treatment by her chil-dren as compared to a father. A man came to Prophet Muhammad (PBUH) and said, "O Allah's Apostle! Who is more entitled to be treated with the best companionship by me?" The Prophet said, "Your mother." The man said. "Who is next?" The Prophet said, "Your mother." The man further said, "Who is next?" The Prophet said, "Your mother." The man asked for the fourth time, "Who is next?" The Prophet said, "Your father." (Sahih Bukhari)

The Prophet Mohammad (PBUH) said, "Look after your mother because your Heaven lies beneath her feet". (Ibn Maja, and Nisai)

Now take the case of daughters and sisters. Prophet Muhammad (PBUH) said, "The one upon whom the trying responsibility of (raising) daughters was placed and he (or she) fulfilled this responsibility in a good manner treating them well, for him (or her) these daughters shall become the means of protection from Hell." (Sahih Bukhari, Sahih Muslim)

Prophet Muhammad (PBUH) said, "Whoever has a girl (daughter, sister, etc) under his guardianship, and he neither buries her alive, nor treats her with contempt, nor give preference to his sons over her, Allah will admit him to Paradise." (Abu Dawood)

Prophet Muhammad (PBUH) said, "A person who raises two daughters until they attain puberty, that man and I will come close to one another on the Day of Resurrection like this. Saying this, the Prophet (PBUH) joined his fingers." (Sahih Muslim)

There are numerous sayings of the Prophet Muhammad (PBUH) regarding good treatment of wives. Even in his last sermon, when the Prophet (PBUH) was giving his last and very important instructions, one key matter advised was regarding good treatment of wives.

On another occasion the Prophet Muhammad (PBUH) said, "The most perfect Muslim in the matter of faith is one who has excellent behaviour; and the best among you are those who behave best towards their wives." (Tirmizi)

The Prophet Muhammad (PBUH) said, "A believer should not be prejudiced towards his believing wife, if he dislikes one of her habits, he may like some other habit." (Sahih Muslim)

The Prophet Muhammad (PBUH) said, "There is a dinar which you spent in the path of Allah, a dinar with which you bought liberty for a slave, a dinar which you gave as charity and a dinar spent on your wife. The most virtuous and rewarding dinar is that one which you spent on your wife." (Sahih Muslim)

According to a Muslim scholar, Shiekh Akram Nadawi, "When she is a daughter, she opens a door of Jannah (Paradise) for her father. When she is a wife, she completes half of the Deen (religion) of her husband. When she is a mother, Jannah (Paradise) lies under her feet – If everyone knew the true status of a Muslim woman in Islam, even the men would want to be women."

The preceding discussion clarifies that according to Islamic teachings, in one area both men and women are equal. In another area, men are given preference over women due to some valid reasons. And in another area, women are given preference over men. This is the kind of beauty and justice that is found in Islamic teachings.

ISLAM AND MUSLIMS

Strictly speaking, Islam and Muslims are two completely distinctive entities. We cannot blame Islam for the bad practices of some Muslims. Once, when the Muslims followed the commandments of Islam, the world was a very different place characterized by peace and justice. For the non-Muslims also it was a Golden Age, one that continued for more than one thousand years. However during this period things gradually kept on degrading starting with the political system. According to the great philosopher-poet of the East, Dr. Allama Iqbal, "During the course of history, the moral and social ideals of Islam have been gradually de-Islamized through the influence of local character, and pre-Islamic superstitions of Muslim nations. These ideals today are more Iranian, Turkish, or Arabian than Islamic. The pure brow of the principal of Tauheed has received, more or less, an impress of heathenish, and the universal and impersonal character of the ethical ideals of Islam has been lost through a process of localization. The only alternative open to us then is to tear off from Islam the hard crust which has immobilized an essentially dynamic outlook on life, and to rediscover the original verities of freedom, equality and solidarity with a view to rebuild our moral, social and political ideals out of their original simplicity and universality." [30]

Many contemporary Muslim societies represent a mixture of Islamic and other cultures, the elements of which may not be Islamic or even may be against the teachings of Islam. Not all the customs and practices in Muslim societies are easy to segregate as Islamic or un-Islamic. One should therefore be very careful in calling each and every practice in a present-day Muslim society as Islamic, without proper investigation.

Sometimes to defame Islam, non-Muslims refer to certain bad practices against women found in some Muslim countries that are not Islamic. Take the case of the Muslim country where I live. There are certain anti-women practices found in certain regions of Pakistan that are completely un-Islamic. Some of these practices are briefly explained below:

Karo Kari:

In this practice, the girl and the boy, when found to have illicit sexual relation, are killed by the family member(s). The boy is called 'Karo' and the girl is called 'Kari'. These killings are done without giving any chance to the boy or the girl to clarify themselves. Data reveals that there are numerous other reasons for such killings which are undertaken on the pretext of Karo Kari.

Honor killing:

According to this custom, when a woman leaves her home and marries a man of her choice, her male family member kills her in the name of honor.

Saam, Swara, and Wani:

Saam, Swara, and Wani are nearly identical practices found in certain regions of Pakistan. According to this custom, if someone is murdered then his tribe or family members or their tribe leader, demands one or more girls from the murderer's tribe or family. Without their consent, these girls are married to any member of the victim's family or victim's tribe. Sometimes the girls are handed over to the other tribe without proper wedding process. These girls are then treated as slaves or as a property of the victim's family.

Watta Satta:

In this custom, when a man marries in another family, then in exchange a woman from the man's family is married to the other family.

Walovar:

According to this practice, which is found in a certain community, the bridegroom gives money to his would-be father-in-law, upon his demand. Marriage cannot take place without such payment. This practice creates many social evils in the society. Marriages are delayed as young men usually do not have the kind of money demanded. After the marriage, the bride usually does not visit her parent's home. The parents also usually avoid visits to the bride's new home. The bride is now considered as if she is the property of her in-laws and they can treat her as they may wish.

Marriage with Holy Quran:

In the case of not finding a suitable match for a woman or in order to prevent giving inheritance to her, an agreement is made between that woman and the Quran. The girl dresses like a bride and sits next to Quran for making this agreement. She is forced to spend the rest of her life like a hermit, away from the joys of the world. She never marries any man like normal girls.

Please note that these corrupt/inhuman/ruthless practices are not common and are not practiced throughout Pakistan. These are only found in certain regions of Pakistan and also are not practiced by all the people living in those regions.

I will quote here the words of a women wing of a Pakistani Islamic political party regarding these practices. After briefly defining these customs and practices, these Islamists write in their brochure:

"The Women Commission Jamat-i-Islami women wing is against all these practices that are not only inhumane but also un-Islamic and demands to put an end to these practices. In order to put an end to these practices, it is necessary to make relevant laws and then enforce those laws. The assembly member of Jamat-i-Islami has put forward a bill against such bad practices in the senate, national, and provincial assemblies, so that the government can seriously make laws on these (matters).

On the other hand, the women killed in Pakistan due to these bad practices as compared to the total population of Pakistan, are much less than the women murdered world over due to violence and other reasons. Unfortunately the picture of Pakistan is portrayed in much exaggerated manner (due to various other reasons).

The position of Jamat-i-Islami women commission of Pakistan on this issue is that the media, education system, and legislative bodies should be used to promote women's respect and honor. It is our real duty to promote awareness of the rights and duties of women in a society and a family that are given by Islam. May Allah accept our efforts for the establishment of a balanced Islamic society. (Amen)" [31] The quoted sentences of an Islamist group will certainly help you believe that how much Islam is against such absurd anti-women practices of some Muslims. As asserted before, Islam is rather the saviour of womankind.

At the end of this topic I would like you to read the following answer given by Dr. Zakir Naik, the world renowned Muslim scholar, for the question, "If Islam is the best religion, why are many of the Muslims dishonest, unreliable, and involved in activities such as cheating, bribing, dealing in drugs, etc.?" The answer to this question as given by Dr. Zakir Naik was: [32]

1. *Media maligns Islam:*-

    a. *Islam is without doubt the best religion but the media is in the hands of the Westerners who are afraid of Islam. The media is continuously broadcasting and printing information against Islam. They either provide misinformation about Islam, misquote Islam or project a point out of proportion, if any.*

    b. *When any bomb blast takes place anywhere, the first people to be accused without proof are invariably the Muslims. This appears as headlines in the news. Later, when they find that non-Muslims were responsible, it appears as insignificant news' item.*

    c. *If a 50-year old Muslim marries a 15-year old girl after taking her permission, it appears on the front page but when a 50-year old non-Muslim rapes a 6-year old girl, it may appear in the news in the inside pages as 'Newsbriefs'. Every day in America on an average 2,713 cases of rape take place but it doesn't appear in the news, since it has become a way of life for the Americans.*

2. *Blacksheep in every community:*- *I am aware that there are some Muslims who are dishonest, unreliable, who cheat, etc. but the media projects this as though only Muslims are involved in such activities. There are blacksheep in every community. I know Muslims who are alcoholics and who can drink most of the non-Muslims under the table.*

3. *Muslims best as a whole:*- *Inspite of all the blacksheep in the Muslim community, Muslims taken on the whole, yet form the best community in the world. We are the biggest community of teetotallers as a whole, i.e. those who don't imbibe alcohol. Collectively, we are a community which gives the maximum charity in the world. There is not a single person in the world who can even show a candle to the Muslims where modesty is concerned; where sobriety is concerned; where human values and ethics are concerned.*

4. Don't judge a car by its driver:- If you want to judge how good is the latest model of the "Mercedes" car and a person who does not know how to drive sits at the steering wheel and bangs up the car, who will you blame? The car or the driver? But naturally, the driver. To analyze how good the car is, a person should not look at the driver but see the ability and features of the car. How fast is it, what is its average fuel consumption, what are the safety measures, etc. Even if I agree for the sake of argument that the Muslims are bad, we can't judge Islam by its followers! If you want to judge how good Islam is then judge it according to its authentic sources, i.e. the Glorious Qur'an and the Sahih Hadith.

5. Judge Islam by its best follower i.e. Prophet Muhammad (pbuh):- If you practically want to check how good a car is, put an expert driver behind the steering wheel. Similarly the best and the most exemplary follower of Islam by whom you can check how good Islam is, is the last and final messenger of God, Prophet Muhammad (pbuh). Besides Muslims, there are several honest and unbiased non-Muslim historians who have acclaimed that prophet Muhammad (pbuh) was the best human being. According to Michael H. Hart who wrote the book, 'The 100 Most Influential Men in History', the topmost position, i.e. the number one position goes to the beloved prophet of Islam, Muhammad (pbuh). There are several such examples of non-Muslims paying great tributes to the prophet (pbuh), like Thomas Carlyle, La-Martine, etc. (By Dr. Zakir Naik)

Chapter 7

Is Islam Against Women?

"... It is even more ironic that most British converts should be women, given the widespread view in the West that Islam treats women poorly. In the United States, women converts outnumber men by four to one..."

(The Times) [1]

Is Islam against women? The answer to this question is definitely 'NO'. However, anyone whose sole source of Islamic knowledge has been the Western media, has a wrong perception that Islam oppresses women. Many non-Muslims especially males, due to their lack of comprehensive understanding about both women and Islam, think that Islam is misogynistic.

As quoted earlier, according to The Times newspaper, "... It is even more ironic that most British converts should be women, given the widespread view in the West that Islam treats women poorly. In the United States, women converts outnumber men by four to one..." My question is; Are these women stupid? These women are coming towards Islam after facing exploitation and injustice in their materialistic cultures. More women are coming towards Islam, a clear proof of the fact that Islam protects women, gives them respect and saves them from exploitation.

We have already understood that men and women are not similar. Islamic teachings hence are different in certain matters with respect to the two genders. However, some Islamic teachings are misquoted by the adversaries of Islam to give a wrong impression. There is a logic and wisdom behind all Islamic teachings that tend to come across as disproportionate. To have a better understanding, the rest of this chapter will discuss some Islamic teachings that differentiate men and women. But first of all I would like to discuss a Hadith of Prophet Muhammad (PBUH) that is mostly quoted by the enemies of Islam to portray a false impression, as if Islam is a misogynistic. The following is the discussion on this Hadith.

WOMEN AND HELL

Prophet Muhammad (PBUH) said: "I was shown the Hell–fire and that the majority of its dwellers were women who were ungrateful." It was asked, "Do they disbelieve in Allah?" (or are they ungrateful to Allah?) He replied, "They are ungrateful to their husbands and are ungrateful for the favors and the good (charitable deeds) done to them. If you have always been good (benevolent) to one of them and then she sees something in you (not of her liking), she will say, 'I have never received any good from you." (Sahih Bukhari)

Well, it is said that either a glass is half empty or it is half full. It all depends upon the person looking at the glass and his or her attitude. A negative person will always say that the glass is half empty and a positive person will always say that the glass is half full. The same is true for this saying of the Holy Prophet (PBUH). People who want to degrade Islam are always looking for an opportunity to find something that can be distorted to portray a false impression about Islam. Such people when they found this hadith, got a golden opportunity for their evil plots, especially in this era when the modern feminist movement is very much present in many parts of the world. Such people always say, "Look! See! Didn't I tell you that Islam is misogynistic. Look at this saying of the Prophet of Islam according to which most women will go to hell." And many people fall into their trap.

I will analyse this saying of the Holy Prophet (PBUH) from an entirely different angle. For the sake of objective analysis, let me give you an analogy. In one of my classes I informed some of my students that I foresee that they will fail the subject as evident from their current and expected future performance. I not only informed them that I foresee that they will fail, but also gave them advice (as a special favour) to help them prepare for exams. Some of them took my advice and cleared the exam. And some of them did not care about my warning and advice and eventually failed. Following are some of the points that are deduced from this analogy:

1. While teaching, I gave them a level field to compete but some were still failing. This does not mean that I wanted them to fail.
2. I informed my students that I foresee them failing. This is a warning for them so that they can show some hard work and ultimately pass.
3. I also gave them a valuable piece of advice to prepare for the exams so that they do not find the exam difficult to pass. This was a special favour of mine for them.
4. Now the students who worked on my advice were wise students because they corrected their behaviour when warned. They ultimately passed the exams.
5. If some students who instead of correcting themselves started saying that the teacher is against them or hates them or wants to fail them, these students were unwise or rather foolish.

Now we will apply this analogy to the saying of the Holy Prophet (PBUH). We will see whether the five points deduced from the analogy can also be applied to the Prophetic saying. According to the Islamic concept, this worldly life for us is nothing but a test. The result of this test will be announced in the hereafter. If we do good deeds then we will go to Paradise. And if we do bad deeds then we will go to Hell.

1. **Does Allah provide women with opportunities to earn paradise as He provides to men?** Definitely yes! Consider the following Ayats from the Holy Quran:
   According to the Holy Quran, "Surely, Muslim men and Muslim women, believing men and believing women, devout men and devout women, truthful men and truthful women, patient men and patient women, humble men and humble women, and the men who give Sadaqah (charity) and the women who give Sadaqah, and the men who fast and the women who fast, and the men who guard their private parts (against evil acts) and the women who guard (theirs), and the men who remember Allah much and the women who remember (Him) – for them, Allah

has prepared forgiveness and a great reward. (Surah Al-Ahzab, Chapter 33, verse 35)

According to the Holy Quran, "Whoever, male or female, does good deeds and is a believer, then such people shall enter Paradise, and they shall not be wronged in the least." (Surah Nisa, Chapter 4, Ayat 124)

According to the Holy Quran, "So, their Lord answered their prayer: I do not allow the labour of any worker from among you, male or female, to go to waste. You are similar to one another. So, those who emigrated, and were expelled from their homes, and were tortured in My way, and fought, and were killed, I shall certainly write off their evil deeds, and shall certainly admit them into gardens beneath which rivers flow, as a reward from Allah. It is Allah with Whom lies the beauty of the reward." (Surah Al-i-Imran, Chapter 3, Ayat 195)

These quoted Quranic statements make it crystal clear that Allah also provides women ample amount of opportunity to earn paradise as provided to men. Women, who will do good deeds like good men, will definitely go to paradise. And the women, who do bad deeds like bad men, will go to hell along with them. It is not so that many women will go to hell just because they are women.

The Prophet Muhammad (PBUH) saw more women in hell and he is mentioning this fact along with the reason for it. If he had seen more men, perhaps he would have also mentioned it. Chances of an exact equal number of men and women in a place are however very remote. Even if I go to a nearby park and count the number of men and women in the park then chances of exact equal numbers is very low. Either men will be more or women will be more. This is more probable.

2. **What is the purpose of warning women?** The purpose of this warning is that women should be careful and do their best to earn paradise.

3. **For helping women, does Prophet Muhammad (PBUH) also give them some good advice?** Yes. As mentioned in the

famous Hadith book of Sahih Muslim, Prophet Muhammad (PBUH) once also said, "O womenfolk, you should give charity and ask much forgiveness for I saw you in bulk amongst the dwellers of Hell." (Sahih Muslim) Thus according to this Hadith, the Prophet (PBUH) advised women to give charity and ask much forgiveness. These are two advices to women so that they can save themselves from going to hell. This is a special favour to women.

4. **Will this advice help women?** Yes, some wise women will definitely take this warning accompanied with advice, positively. They will become more careful and start work according to the given advice. Thus they will ultimately be saved from hell. This warning and advice will turn out to be a blessing for them.

    Some men after knowing this warning for women will also become careful and ask Allah s.w.t for forgiveness for their wives when they are ingrate. I am writing this because I know a Muslim man who whenever he is unhappy with his wife, due to her ingrate attitude, prays to Allah, "O Allah! I have forgiven her. You also forgive her." He says this out of his love for his wife.

5. **Will this advice not help women?** Yes some inane women (and men) will take this warning negatively. Some women will make it an ego issue. And some men and women will take it as a golden opportunity to defame the beautiful religion of Islam. Instead of taking this warning for their benefit, they will keep on perceiving and portraying Islam as misogynistic. In this way they will further become eligible for hell.

EARNING LIVELIHOOD

Current literature on modern management talks a lot about the concept of 'Specialization' and its benefits. People say that this era is the era of 'specialization'. However people tend to reject this concept when they come across the idea of specialized roles of men and women in a society.

There are two fundamental instincts in all living creatures namely 'Preservation of the Self' and 'Preservation of the Species'. Women differ from men both physically and psychologically. One can say that men and women are not similar. Allah s.w.t has therefore given the various responsibilities to men and women in a society that are more compatible with their talents and abilities. Men have been given the primary responsibility of 'Preservation of the Self' that is earning livelihood, defend against enemies and so on. Similarly women have been given the primary responsibility of 'Preservation of the Species' that is child care, upbringing future generations, and so on.

A very big favor by Islam to women is that, although she can earn money, the burden of earning the livelihood is not on her shoulders. She has no financial obligation to support her family. During her whole life, Allah has made a man, in the form of a father, a brother, a husband, or a son, responsible for fulfilling all her material needs with full respect. This is her legal right which she can claim at a court against her nearest relative. And if she has no relative to look after her then she can claim her livelihood from the state. The court shall provide and guarantee her livelihood regularly from the public exchequer.

In most modern cultures, she has no choice but to take part in the tiring money earning activities. This is not fair to her. Renowned Islamic scholar Dr. Ghulam Murtaza Malik (late) explains, "Let us be honest with ourselves. Man cannot replace woman. Woman has got some duties imposed on her by nature. These duties cannot be done by a man. But man is very selfish. He wants her to do these duties, all right. And along with these duties, he wants her to come out of her house and earn livelihood of men... I ask my dear (male) friends, 'Can you do all those jobs which a woman does? Can a male keep a child in his womb for nine months? Can you give birth to a child? Can you suffer all what a women suffers? Can you love a child as a woman does? Can you keep awake yourself for the whole night as woman does? Has the man got the patience, the love, those sentiments, those feelings as the mother has for her child? Can you do all these sacrifices which a woman does for the sake of her child? Can you train a baby just in the same way as the mother does? ... He does not have the patience. He cannot keep himself awake for the whole night for the sake of his children... Now it is the selfishness of man that he could not replace women, and he kept the duties of women to the woman and also imposed upon her the duties of the men which did not belong to her, which actually belonged to men. Going to the market, working in the field, going for job are not the jobs of a woman. What you call emancipation of woman today in Europe or America is not emancipation of women. It is exploitation." [2]

Women also find it difficult to work during her days of pregnancy, child birth, and menstrual cycles. It is also difficult for her to manage work when she has small kids to take care of. She suffers from various physical and emotional problems due to these events. It is advisable for her to remain comfortable at home during these days. A lady doctor during a UNDP gender sensitivity training said that she would love to quit her job and stay at home if she had a choice to do so. [3]

Women who choose to work outside their homes have a set of problems to face. The problems faced are at the actual workplace, at home, and in between the two places. In chapter two of this book, I have discussed in detail with concrete facts and figures, the following problems faced by working women:

- Discrimination
- Sexual harassment
- Increased responsibilities
- Neglected children
- Greedy family members
- Problems on the way

Someone once asked me, "What will happen if half of our population (females) will not take part in the economic activity?" The spontaneous reply was, "Then the unemployment problem of the other half (males) would be resolved." Unemployment is a big problem throughout the world. According to an International Labor Organization 'World Employment Report', "The current unemployment situation represents an enormous waste of resources and an unacceptable level of human suffering. It has led to growing social exclusion, rising inequality…and a host of social ills." [4]

One argument given by some people is that these days it is necessary for both husband and wife to earn in order to maintain their current lifestyle. We know that there are not many jobs available in the job market. Suppose there are two families and there are two jobs available in the market. There can be two cases in such a situation. Case number one is that both jobs go to the husband and wife of the same family. Case number two is that the husbands of both families get each job. What is a better option from the economic and social point of view? Case number one would result in unbalanced distribution of wealth in a society. There is a higher probability that case number two will prevent many suicides of males who are unable to make both ends meet for their families. Newspapers are regularly reporting such suicides in our society.

Some might argue that there is a shortage of labour in many developed countries. In these countries women also work and still they have to import labor from abroad. If women were to concentrate more on the role of reproducing and upbringing the labor force, there may be a considerable impact on resolving the labour shortage problem in the near future. This would be a great service indeed for their society. Their current full employment is not resolving the problem and it is forcasted to worsen in the future. Realizing this, many developed countries including Japan are now encouraging families to have more kids by offering them incentives but people are not ready to do so due to their new lifestyle.

As quoted earlier, Dr. Henry Makow in his article 'Debauchery of American Womenhood' writes, "Feminism teaches woman that feminine nature has resulted in 'oppression' and that she should convert to male behavior instead. The result: a confused and aggressive woman with a large chip on her shoulder, unfit to become a wife or mother. This, of course, is the goal of the social engineers at the NWO: undermine sexual identity and destroy the family, create social and personal dysfunction and reduce population." [5] What Mr. Makow is saying about population is well supported by statistical data. Studies in a broad spectrum of developing countries have provided strong support for the argument that high female employment opportunities outside their home is also associated increasingly with lower levels of fertility.

Once a financially well-off foreign national posed a surprising question, "Adeel, What do you think? Is it necessary to have children?" These nations are aging and dying with time.

Some people in Europe are now even using the theme of 'fear' to motivate people for having children. For example in a research documentary by the title of 'The world is changing' [6], the world's changing demographics is shown for various regions. According to this documentary if any culture wants to maintain itself for more than 25 years then its fertility rate should be atleast 2.11 children/family. Historically, a culture has never reversed its dying process with a fertility rate of 1.9 children/family. And this process is impossible to reverse at the fertility rate 1.3 children/family. According to this documentary, as of the year 2007, the fertility rate of various countries are: 1.8 for France, 1.6 for England, 1.3 for Greece, 1.3 for Germany, 1.2 for Italy, 1.1 for Spain, and 1.6 for Canada. The fertility rate for the entire European Union combined is 1.38. Therefore, surely these civilizations will eventually cease to exist with the passage of time. This is not the trend however in Muslim countries.

To reiterate, a very big favor of Islam on women is that, although she can earn money, the burden of earning the livelihood is not on her shoulders. She has no financial obligation to support her family. However, it must also be mentioned that there are occasions due to which a woman has to go out from her home to earn the livelihood e.g. there is no one to fulfill her financial needs. Whenever a female leaves her home, she must adhere to the laws of Hijaab. It is the responsibility of the Muslim community to organize work for women, so that she can do so as per the Muslim cultural atmosphere, where her rights are respected. Some areas where women can easily enter into the workforce are home industry, primary education, female colleges/universities, female hospitals/clinics, etc.

Ms. Annie Besant (1847–1933), a prominent British theosophist, women's rights activist, writer and orator, writes in her book, "...Those things are forgotten while people are hypnotized by the words of monogamy and polygamy and do not look at what lies behind it in the West – the frightful degradation of women who are thrown into the streets when their first protectors, weary of them, no longer give them any assistance." [7]

This is indeed the selfishness of the males. Homemaking in itself is an honourable and serious responsibility. It is the foundation on which healthy societies can be built. Societies that disrespect homemaking, lose the homemakers which results in broken homes as can be witnessed in many parts of the world. It should be recognized that the trend to belittle the task of homemaking is anti-family and anti-society and must be curbed. Initially women all over the world were not doing jobs like today. The scene began to change in the 19th century, not under the force of a moral argument, but because of pressures generated by industrial revolution. The juggernaut of the industrial revolution destroyed the old handicraft based economy and forced workers to move to sweat shops in big cities where industries were. Workers demanded, in vain, 'family wages' so a man could support his family on his income. The capitalists would rather have the family also come to their service if they wanted to be fed. There was no option for the people but to send the women to the factory to make ends meet.

Later, the opening of clerical jobs needed millions of other women to come out of their houses and become secretaries, sales girls, typists, and waitresses. It was 'cheap labor' indeed. The process was given a moral purpose by the language of the feminists. It measured women's progress by how many had been driven out of their homes. It labeled the social upheavals caused by the industrial revolution as women's emancipation. According to its convoluted logic if a woman serves food to her husband and children, it is slavery. If she provides the same service to total strangers in a restaurant or aircraft, risking their never ending advances, that is emancipation!

For more elaboration of the topic, I am reproducing here an article 'Home, Sweet Home' by Mr. Khalid Baig on this topic of women employment and its affect in Western societies. Following is his article:

Home, Sweet Home [8]

"My own feeling is that we've pushed women too far," says Dr. T. Berry Brazelton, the 80 year old Harvard University doctor who is frequently called "America's Paediatrician," in a recent interview in the Los Angeles Times. "We've split them in two, and we have not given them back anything to support themselves on either end." He has witnessed what forcing the women into the workforce and the breakdown of the family have done to the American children. "I just think our country is in deep, deep trouble," he agonizes.

Opinion leaders of all persuasions agree. Ask America's First Lady, who considers herself a champion of women's and children's causes. In her 1996 book, "It Takes a Village," she offers this assessment: "… children's potential lost to spirit-crushing poverty, children's health lost to unaffordable care, children's hearts lost in divorce and custody fights, children's futures lost in an overburdened foster care system, children's lives lost to abuse and violence, our society lost to itself as we fail our children." This is a society in which by her account: "homicide and suicide kill almost seven thousand children every year; one in four of all children are born to unmarried mothers, many of whom are children themselves; and 135,000 children bring guns to school each day. Children in every social stratum suffer from abuse, neglect, and preventable emotional problems." She also approvingly quotes: "If you bungle raising your children, I don't think whatever else you do matters very much." It is obvious that America as a nation, has bungled this thoroughly.

Welcome to the dark side of "Women's Emancipation." Today women are free in America. Free from the protection of a home and the support of a husband who would be responsible to provide for them. They are on their own. In turn, the children have been freed from the rigidities of the traditional home, where father and mother provide for them, take care of them, and guide them. The children are also on their own. Just in case they do not like it, the society has been experimenting with all kinds of poultry farms ---day care they call them---to take care of them.

Things have gone so wrong for so long that everyone has lost all hope that the society can rectify it completely and retrace its steps. Hillary Clinton admits: "My personal wish, that every child has an intact, dependable family, will likely remain a wish." So, she is just trying to build a better poultry farm with the help of the whole village. Dr. Brazelton knows that the children need the mother at home. "I think you are giving a gift to the child when you stay home with him as long as you can." However, he knows that it cannot be very long, as, to stay home, "being just a mother," is not good enough any more. He knows the psychological crisis faced by the stay-at-home mothers, so he pleads with everyone to do as much as they can.

Now contrast this with the U.N. edict that the women in the rest of the world, especially the Muslim world, must take up all kinds of jobs outside the home; that the goal should be their total economic independence. In other words, women must be forced outside the home so they are no longer available to take care of the children within the home. They must be "liberated" from the home, so they can enjoy the same fruits of "emancipation" as the women are "enjoying" in the U.S.

The destruction of the family in America, or the West in general, was not planned. It just happened as a logical result of the materialistic, hedonistic, Godless civilizational values that have gripped these societies. But the U.N. decree that the rest of the world must follow the same disastrous path, is something else. It is as if a person lost an eye to horseplay, and now wants everyone else to voluntarily have an eye removed!

It is unconscionable that we should be answering such chicanery with apologetics of the kind that normally begin with, "Islam also allows women to," as in, "Islam also allows women to work outside the home." Yes, it does in case of necessity, but that is beside the point. The real issue is that Islam frees a wife from the burden to provide for the family. It is solely the husband's responsibility. In return, the wife's main responsibility is to stay home and take care of the children.

The primary field of women's endeavor is the home, sweet home. And this has to be stated without hesitation or apology. The Qur'an says: "And stay quietly in your homes."[Al-Ahzab, 33:33]. And the Prophet, Sall-Allahu alayhi wa sallam, said: "The wife is responsible for taking care of the home of her husband, and she will be accountable for those given in her charge."[Bukhari, Muslim]. This is also the most rewarding job that anyone can think of. The Prophet, Sall-Allahu alayhi wa sallam, assured the woman who stays home to take care of the children, that she would be with him in paradise. According to another hadith, during pregnancy and the entire period of nursing, the believing mother is like the soldier on active duty. If she dies, she gets the reward reserved for a martyr. Yet another hadith says to the women: "Take care of the home. That is your jihad." [Musnad Ahmad].

All of these clearly establish the basic division of labor between men and women according to Islam: men are responsible for the affairs outside the home and the women are responsible for taking care of the home. This division is not a relic of some dark past. It is the only basis on which a healthy society has ever been built and can be built today. The nations that have tried to alter this natural arrangement long enough have nothing but grief and trouble to show for their efforts. And they seem to be groping in the dark, unable to undo the damage and get out of the quagmire. Is there any sane reason that those who have the Light should follow them on the dark highway to disaster? (by Khalid Baig)

WOMEN'S DRESSING

Prophet Muhammad (PBUH) said, "There are over seventy branches of faith, of which the greatest is to say, 'There is no god but Allah', and the most paltry is to remove filth from the path. And modesty is also a part of faith." (Sahih Bukhari, Sahih Muslim)

Islam does not believe in objectification of women. It prescribes a modest dress code for men and especially women. Women who observe the Islamic dress code do not feel oppressed but some Western and so called liberal people feel this way about them. These people think that Muslim women, as they have to wear some extra clothes, are oppressed.

On the other hand many Muslim women feel that Western women are oppressed and are being objectified due to their skin tight short immodest dressings. Nicholas D. Kristof and Sheryl Wu Dunn write in their book, "Westerners sometimes feel sorry for Muslim women in the way that leaves them uncomfortable, even angry. When Nick quizzed a group of female Saudi doctors and nurses in Riyadh about women's rights, they bristled. 'Why do foreigners always ask about clothing?' one woman doctor asked, 'Why does it matter so much what we wear. Of all the issues in the world, is that really important?' Another said: 'You think we're victims, because we cover our hair and wear modest clothing. But we think that it's Western women who are repressed, because they have to show their bodies – even go through surgery to change their bodies – to please men." [9]

The objective of Islamic modest dressing is not to restrict the liberty of women, but to protect them from harm and molestation. In the East and in the West, a distinctive public dress of some sort or another has always been a badge of honor or distinction, both among men and women. This can be traced back on the earliest civilizations. Assyrian Law in its palmiest days (say, 7th century B.C), enjoined the veiling of married women and forbade the veiling of slaves and women of ill fame. According to Bible, "... And every women who prays and prophesies with her head uncovered dishonors her head..." (1 Corinthians 11:3-6). "I also want women to dress modestly, with decency and propriety, with not braided hair or gold or pearls or expensive clothes, but with good deeds, appropriate for women who profess to worship God." (1 Timothy 2:9-10)

The following incident took place when world renowned boxer Muhammad Ali's daughters arrived at his home wearing clothes that were not modest. This story as told by one of his daughters is: "When we finally arrived, the chauffeur escorted my younger sister, Laila, and me up to my father's suite. As usual, he was hiding behind the door waiting to scare us. We exchanged many hugs and kisses as we could possibly give in one day. My father took a good look at us. Then he sat me down on his lap and said something that I will never forget. He looked me straight in the eyes and said, 'Hana, everything that God made valuable in the world is covered and hard to get to. Where do you find diamonds? Deep down in the ground, covered and protected. Where do you find pearls? Deep down at the bottom of the ocean, covered up and protected in a beautiful shell. Where do you find gold? Way down in the mine, covered over with layers and layers of rock. You've got to work hard to get to them.' He looked at me with serious eyes. 'Your body is sacred. You're far more precious than diamonds and pearls, and you should be covered too.'" [10]

According to the Holy Quran, "Tell the believing men that they must lower their gazes and guard their private parts; it is more decent for them. Surely Allah is All-Aware of what they do. And tell the believing women that they must lower their gazes and guard their private parts, and must not expose their adornment, except that which appears thereof, and must wrap their bosoms with their shawls, and must not expose their adornment, except to their husbands or their fathers or the fathers of their husbands, or to their sons or the sons of their husbands, or to their brothers or the sons of their brothers or the sons of their sisters, or to their women, or to those owned by their right hands, or male attendants having no (sexual) urge, or to the children who are not yet conscious of the shames of women. And let them not stamp their feet in a way that the adornment they conceal is known. And repent to Allah O believers, all of you, so that you may achieve success." (Surah An-Noor, Chapter 24, Ayat 30-31)

Allah s.w.t also says in Holy Quran, "O Prophet! Tell thy wives and daughters and the believing women that they should cast their outer garments over their persons (when abroad): that is most convenient that they should be known (as such) and not molested: and Allah is Oft-Forgiving Most Merciful." (Surah Al-Ahzab, Chapter 33, Ayat 59)

These days even in Muslim societies we see such women who are although dressed-up, their clothes do not serve the purpose. Their revealing clothes actually highlight their various body parts that are meant to be concealed. Following are some of the sayings of the Holy Prophet (PBUH) regarding such women:

"Women who are naked even though they are wearing clothes, go astray and make others go astray, and they will not enter the Garden (paradise) and they will not find its scent, and its scent is experienced from as far as the distance travelled in five hundred years." (Muwatta)

"There are two types, amongst the denizens of Hell, I have yet not seen them. One possessing whips like the tail of an ox and they flog people with them. (The second one) the women who would be naked in spite of their being dressed, who are seduced (to wrong paths) and seduce others with their hair high like humps. These women would not get into Paradise and they would not perceive the odour of Paradise, although its fragrance can be perceived from such and such distance (from great distance)." (Sahih Muslim)

Sara Bokker is a former actress/model/fitness instructor and activist in USA. In her following article, she is sharing her experiences of becoming a Muslim and her observance of the Islamic dress code for women.

Why I Shed Bikini for Niqab: The New Symbol of Women's Liberation [11]

I am an American woman who was born in the midst of America's "Heartland." I grew up, just like any other girl, being fixated with the glamour of life in "the big city." Eventually, I moved to Florida and on to South Beach of Miami, a hotspot for those seeking the "glamorous life." Naturally, I did what most average Western girls do. I focused on my appearance and appeal, basing my self-worth on how much attention I got from others. I worked out religiously and became a personal trainer, acquired an upscale waterfront residence, became a regular "exhibiting" beach-goer and was able to attain a "living-in-style" kind of life.

Years went by, only to realize that my scale of self-fulfillment and happiness slid down the more I progressed in my "feminine appeal." I was a slave to fashion. I was a hostage to my looks.

As the gap continued to progressively widen between my self-fulfillment and lifestyle, I sought refuge in escapes from alcohol and parties to meditation, activism, and alternative religions, only to have the little gap widen to what seemed like a valley. I eventually realized it all was merely a pain killer rather than an effective remedy.

By now it was September 11, 2001. As I witnessed the ensuing barrage on Islam, Islamic values and culture, and the infamous declaration of the "new crusade," I started to notice something called Islam. Up until that point, all I had associated with Islam was women covered in "tents," wife beaters, harems, and a world of terrorism.

As a feminist libertarian, and an activist who was pursuing a better world for all, my path crossed with that of another activist who was already at the lead of indiscriminately furthering causes of reform and justice for all. I joined in the ongoing campaigns of my new mentor which included, at the time, election reform and civil rights, among others. Now my new activism was fundamentally different. Instead of "selectively" advocating justice only to some, I learned that ideals such as justice, freedom, and respect are meant to be and are essentially universal, and that own good and common good are not in conflict. For the first time, I knew what "all people are created equal" really means. But most importantly, I learned that it only takes faith to see the world as one and to see the unity in creation.

One day I came across a book that is negatively stereotyped in the West--The Holy Qur'an. I was first attracted by the style and approach of the Qur'an, and then intrigued by its outlook on existence, life, creation, and the relationship between Creator and creation. I found the Qur'an to be a very insightful address to heart and soul without the need for an interpreter or pastor.

Eventually I hit a moment of truth: my new-found self-fulfilling activism was nothing more than merely embracing a faith called Islam where I could live in peace as a "functional" Muslim.

I bought a beautiful long gown and head cover resembling the Muslim woman's dress code and I walked down the same streets and neighborhoods where only days earlier I had walked in my shorts, bikini, or "elegant" western business attire. Although the people, the faces, and the shops were all the same, one thing was remarkably distinct--I was not--nor was the peace at being a woman I experienced for the very first time. I felt as if the chains had been broken and I was finally free. I was delighted with the new looks of wonder on people's faces in place of the looks of a hunter watching his prey I had once sought. Suddenly a weight had been lifted off my shoulders. I no longer spent all my time consumed with shopping, makeup, getting my hair done, and working out. Finally, I was free.

Of all places, I found my Islam at the heart of what some call "the most scandalous place on earth," which makes it all the more dear and special.

While content with Hijab I became curious about Niqab, seeing an increasing number of Muslim women in it. I asked my Muslim husband, whom I married after I reverted to Islam, whether I should wear Niqab or just settle for the Hijab I was already wearing. My husband simply advised me that he believes Hijab is mandatory in Islam while Niqab is not. At the time, my Hijab consisted of head scarf that covered all my hair except for my face, and a loose long black gown called "Abaya" that covered all my body from neck to toe.

A year-and-a-half passed, and I told my husband I wanted to wear Niqab. My reason, this time, was that I felt it would be more pleasing to Allah, the Creator, increasing my feeling of peace at being more modest. He supported my decision and took me to buy an "Isdaal," a loose black gown that covers from head to toe, and Niqab, which covers all my head and face except for my eyes.

Soon enough, news started breaking about politicians, Vatican clergymen, libertarians, and so-called human rights and freedom activists condemning Hijab at times, and Niqab at others as being oppressive to women, an obstacle to social integration, and more recently, as an Egyptian official called it—"a sign of backwardness."

I find it to be a blatant hypocrisy when Western governments and so-called human rights groups rush to defend woman's rights when some governments impose a certain dress code on women, yet such "freedom fighters" look the other way when women are being deprived of their rights, work, and education just because they choose to exercise their right to wear Niqab or Hijab. Today, women in Hijab or Niqab are being increasingly barred from work and education not only under totalitarian regimes such as in Tunisia, Morocco, and Egypt, but also in Western democracies such as France, Holland, and Britain.

Today I am still a feminist, but a Muslim feminist, who calls on Muslim women to assume their responsibilities in providing all the support they can for their husbands to be good Muslims. To raise their children as upright Muslims so they may be beacons of light for all humanity once again. To enjoin good--any good--and to forbid evil--any evil. To speak righteousness and to speak up against all ills. To fight for our right to wear Niqab or Hijab and to please our Creator whichever way we chose. But just as importantly to carry our experience with Niqab or Hijab to fellow women who may never have had the chance to understand what wearing Niqab or Hijab means to us and why do we, so dearly, embrace it.

Most of the women I know wearing Niqab are Western reverts, some of whom are not even married. Others wear Niqab without full support of either family or surroundings. What we all have in common is that it is the personal choice of each and every one of us, which none of us is willing to surrender.

Willingly or unwillingly, women are bombarded with styles of "dressing-in-little-to-nothing" virtually in every means of communication everywhere in the world. As an ex non-Muslim, I insist on women's right to equally know about Hijab, its virtues, and the peace and happiness it brings to a woman's life as it did to mine. Yesterday, the bikini was the symbol of my liberty, when in actuality it only liberated me from my spirituality and true value as a respectable human being.

I couldn't be happier to shed my bikini in South Beach and the "glamorous" Western lifestyle to live in peace with my Creator and enjoy living among fellow humans as a worthy person. It is why I choose to wear Niqab, and why I will die defending my inalienable right to wear it. Today, Niqab is the new symbol of woman's liberation.

To women who surrender to the ugly stereotype against the Islamic modesty of Hijab, I say: You don't know what you are missing. (by Sara Bokker)

Following are some of the portions from an article 'Veil: The View from the Inside' by a Japanese woman, Nakata Khaula, who converted to Islam in France and started to observe Hijab:

"Anyone whose sole source of knowledge about Islam has been the Western media, 'knows' that Islam 'oppresses' women. The hijab or veil, is the symbol of such 'oppression.' To 'liberate' Muslim women from such 'oppression' has been the cherished goal of media pundits, Western 'experts' on Islam, and the feminists. Such is the result of a fierce propaganda campaign that has been going on for a very long time. The attack has been so ferocious that the veil and all the aspects of Shariah (Islamic laws) dealing with women should have pulverized under its intense heat. Yet in the U.S., the Western Europe, Japan and Australia, it is the women who have been turning to Islam in record numbers. It was not supposed to happen! And when it does, the propaganda machinery does not acknowledge it. It just puts a little more pressure on the accelerator.

There is something to be said about the N.Y. Times or L.A. Times reporter who will travel half way around the world to interview a woman with a Muslim sounding name in, say, Pakistan to talk about the Shariah's injustices to the women, while ignoring the Muslim women in their own backyard who have experienced both worlds and love the Islamic one --- hijab and all. The reporter travels not in search of truth, but only believability. For, the truth hurts; believability, on the other hand, is the foundation for building circulation and for propaganda.

Should not we listen to the woman who was raised and educated in the west, had first hand experience of the status of women in this society, then studied Islam and observed the life behind the veil, decided to cross the fence against all the propaganda about immediate doom, and has enjoyed life ever since? That woman does not exist in the propaganda world. She is never allowed to speak on the pages of "prestigious" publications. She has no rights! She is the one you should be listening to, to find the truth. She speaks on these pages. Listen to her. ....

The feeling still persists amongst non-Muslims that Muslim women wear the hijab simply because they are slaves to tradition, so much so that it is seen as a symbol of oppression. Women's liberation and independence is, so they believe, impossible unless they first remove the hijab.

Such naivete is shared by 'Muslims' with little or no knowledge of Islam. Being so used to secularism and religious eclecticism, pick and mix, they are unable to comprehend that Islam is universal and eternal. This apart, women all over the world, non-Arabs, are embracing Islam and wearing the hijab as a religious requirement, not a misdirected sense of "tradition." I am but one example of such women. My hijab is not a part of my racial or traditional identity; it has no social or political significance; it is, purely and simply, my religious identity.

For non-Muslims, the hijab not only covers a woman's hair, but also hides something, leaving them no access. They are being excluded from something which they have taken for granted in secular society. I have worn the hijab since embracing Islam in Paris.... As a foreigner in Paris, I sometimes felt uneasy about being stared at by men. In my hijab I went unnoticed, protected from impolite stares....

I often wonder why people say nothing about the veil of the Catholic nun but criticize vehemently the veil of a Muslimah, regarding it as a symbol of "terrorism" and "oppression." I did not mind abandoning colorful clothes in favor of black; in fact, I had always had a sense of longing for the religious lifestyle of a nun even before becoming a Muslimah! ...

I heard one girl telling her friend that I was a Buddhist nun; how similar a Muslimah, a Buddhist nun and a Christian nun are! Once, on a train, the elderly man next to me asked why I was dressed in such unusual fashion. When I explained that I was a Muslimah and that Islam commands women to cover their bodies so as not to trouble men who are weak and unable to resist temptation, he seemed impressed. When he left the train he thanked me and said that he would have liked more time to speak to me about Islam. ...

My father was worried when I went out in long sleeves and a head-cover even in the hottest weather, but I found that my hijab protected me from the sun. Indeed, it was I who also felt uneasy looking at my younger sister's legs while she wore short pants. I have often been embarrassed, even before declaring Islam, by the sight of a woman's bosoms and hips clearly outlined by tight, thin clothing. I felt as if I was seeing some-thing secret. If such a sight embarrasses me, one of the same sex, it is not difficult to imagine the effect on men. In Islam, men and women are commanded to dress modestly and not be naked in public, even in all male or all female situations. ...

The way people walk around naked (or almost so), excreting or making love in public, robs them of the sense of shame and reduces them to the status of animals. In Japan, *women only wear makeup when they go out and have little regard for how they look at home. In Islam a wife will try to look beautiful for her husband and her husband will try to look good for his wife. There is modesty even between husband and wife and this embellishes the relationship.*

Muslims are accused of being over-sensitive about the human body but the degree of sexual harassment which occurs these days justifies modest dress. Just as a short skirt can send the signal that the wearer is available to men, so the hijab signals, loud and clear: "I am forbidden for you...

Once accustomed to, the niqab is certainly not inconvenient. In fact I felt like the owner of a secret masterpiece, a treasure which you can neither know about, nor see. Whereas non-Muslims may think they are life imitating caricatures when they see Muslim couples walk in the streets, the oppressed, and the oppressor, the possessed, and the possessor, the reality is that the women feel like queens being led by servants. ...

It is an error of judgment to think that a Muslim woman covers herself because she is a private possession of her husband. In fact, she preserves her dignity and refuses to be possessed by strangers. It is non-Muslim (and "liberated" Muslim) women who are to be pitied for displaying their private self for all to see. ...

An outsider may see Islam as restricting Muslims. In side, however, there is peace, freedom, and joy, which those who experience it have never known before. Practicing Muslims, whether those born in Muslim families or those returned to Islam, choose Islam rather than the illusory freedom of secular life. If it oppresses women, why are so many well-educated young women in Europe, America, Japan, Australia, indeed all over the world, abandoning "liberty" and "independence" and embracing Islam?

A person blinded by prejudice may not see it, but a woman in hijab is as brightly beautiful as an angel, full of self-confidence, serenity, and dignity. No signs of oppression scar her face. 'For indeed it is not the eyes that grow blind, but it is the hearts within the bosoms, that grow blind,' says the Qur'an (Al-Hajj 22:46). How else can we explain the great gap in understanding between us and such people? [12] *(by Nakata Khaula)*

SEGREGATION OF THE SEXES

Islam disallows the free mixing of the two sexes. Allah s.w.t has put strong sexual desires in each one of us. It is even said by some that a man is a sexual animal. These intense sexual feelings were necessary for the continuation of the human race.

As sexual feelings are intense therefore there is a very high chance for its corruption as evident from the following figures regarding women working in US forces with their male colleagues: "The Pentagon's latest figures show that nearly 3,000 women were sexually assaulted in fiscal year 2008, up 9% from the year before; among women serving in Iraq and Afghanistan, the number rose 25%...The problem is even worse than that. The Pentagon estimates that 80% to 90% of sexual assaults go unreported, and it's no wonder." [13]

Another Time Magazine article 'When the Date Turns into Rape', informs about the phenomenon of 'date rape'. This article mentions, "Susan, now 22 and a college senior, was raped almost three years ago on a first date. She met the man in a cafeteria at summer school and went to his dorm that evening to watch television news and get acquainted. After 45 minutes of chitchat about national affairs, he began pawing and kissing her, ignoring her pleas to stop. 'You really don't want me to stop,' he said, and forced her to have sex. The attack was an all too familiar incident of date rape. Like many victims, Susan was unwary and alone too soon with a man she barely..." [14]

Unlike the perception of some, many sex crimes are committed by individuals whom a woman knows like her family member or her boyfriend. According to the feminist organization: "Rape is more likely to be committed by someone we know than by a stranger. Contrary to common stereotypes, the vast majority of rapes occur between members of the same racial group. Most rapists lead everyday lives, go to school, work, and have families and friends. ...You may experience loss in many ways. For many women, rape or abuse may have conflicted with our ideas of whom we can trust or where we are safe." [15] This means that a woman needs to be also careful with people close to her.

The feminist organization mentions the after-effects of a sexual crime committed against a woman: "…Throughout the healing process, you may experience grief over parts of your life that you felt you missed. Some survivors talk about a loss of innocence or a loss of their sense of power. 'I feel like a part of me died, like my life will never be the same. Because I was raped by my boyfriend as a teen, I feel like I missed the chance to have a normal adolescence when everyone says those should have been the best years of my life'." [16]

It is said that it is better to be safe rather than sorry. Some safety recommendations as prescribed by the feminist organization are:

"The most effective protection comes from being with other women. Arrange to walk home together."

"…Walk in the middle of the street, avoiding dark places and groups of men." "Avoid groups of men on public transportation."

"If you can possibly avoid it, don't hitchhike; it is just too dangerous." [17]

These recommendations by a pure secular feminist organization are again pointing towards segregation of the two sexes for women's safety.

The foregoing discussion was mainly on sex without a woman's consent. However the case where her consent exists is also not good for her and the whole society. As mentioned before in this book, according to the newspaper daily Mail of UK: "Nearly a quarter of all abortions in Britain are carried out on girls under the age of 20, a major report has revealed… The data, compiled by the REPROSTAT group, the EU's community health monitoring programme, details abortion figures across the region. Most of the figures are for 2008, but the data is slightly older for several countries. The report shows some 1.2 million terminations are carried out a year – the equivalent of the populations of member countries Malta and Cyprus combined." [18]

We already have had a detailed discussion on this topic in Chapter 5. These are all the bitter fruits of un-segregated societies. Islam does not allow such things to happen in a Islamic society. That is why Islam restricts free mixing of the sexes. The purpose is to keep the spark away from the fuel. Islam however encourages people to marry and satisfy their sexual desires legally through the process of marriage where both man and woman also serve their full responsibilities as laid down upon them in their role as a spouse.

Following is the full version of the TIME magazine article by Nancy Gibbs that was quoted in the preceding discussion. The article depicts the ruthless behaviour of fellow men towards their female colleagues working in the US army:

Sexual Assaults on Female Soldiers: Don't Ask, Don't Tell

What does it tell us that female soldiers deployed overseas stop drinking water after 7 p.m. to reduce the odds of being raped if they have to use the bathroom at night? Or that a soldier who was assaulted when she went out for a cigarette was afraid to report it for fear she would be demoted — for having gone out without her weapon? Or that, as Representative Jane Harman puts it, "a female soldier in Iraq is more likely to be raped by a fellow soldier than killed by enemy fire."

The fight over "Don't ask, don't tell" made headlines this winter as an issue of justice and history and the social evolution of our military institutions. We've heard much less about another set of hearings in the House Armed Services Committee. Maybe that's because too many commanders still don't ask, and too many victims still won't tell, about the levels of violence endured by women in uniform. (See TIME's special report on the state of the American woman.)

The Pentagon's latest figures show that nearly 3,000 women were sexually assaulted in fiscal year 2008, up 9% from the year before; among women serving in Iraq and Afghanistan, the number rose 25%. When you look at the entire universe of female

veterans, close to a third say they were victims of rape or assault while they were serv-
ing — twice the rate in the civilian population.

The problem is even worse than that. The Pentagon estimates that 80% to 90% of
sexual assaults go unreported, and it's no wonder. Anonymity is all but impossible;
a Government Accountability Office report concluded that most victims stay silent
because of "the belief that nothing would be done; fear of ostracism, harassment, or
ridicule; and concern that peers would gossip." More than half feared they would be
labeled troublemakers. A civilian who is raped can get confidential, or "privileged,"
advice from her doctors, lawyers, victim advocates; the only privilege in the military
applies to chaplains. A civilian who knows her assailant has a much better chance of
avoiding him than does a soldier at a remote base, where filing charges can be a career
killer — not for the assailant but the victim. Women worry that they will be removed
from their units for their own "protection" and talk about not wanting to undermine
their missions or the cohesion of their units. And then some just do the math: only
8% of cases that are investigated end in prosecution, compared with 40% for civilians
arrested for sex crimes. Astonishingly, about 80% of those convicted are honorably
discharged nonetheless.

The sense of betrayal runs deep in victims who joined the military to be part of a loyal
team pursuing a larger cause; experts liken the trauma to incest and the particular
damage done when assault is inflicted by a member of the military "family." Women
are often denied claims for posttraumatic stress caused by the assault if they did not
bring charges at the time. There are not nearly enough mental-health professionals in
the system to help them. Female vets are four times more likely to be homeless than
male vets are, according to the Service Women's Action Network, and of those,
40% report being victims of sexual assault.

Experts offer many theories for the causes: that military culture is intrinsically vio-
lent and hypermasculine, that the military is slow to identify potential risks among
raw young recruits, that too many commanders would rather look the other way than
acknowledge a breakdown in their units, that it has simply not been made a high
enough priority. "A lot of my male colleagues believe that the only thing a general needs
to worry about is whether he can win a war," says Congresswoman Loretta Sanchez

of the Armed Services Committee. "People are not taking this seriously. Commanding officers in the field are not understanding how important this is."

But there are some signs that both Congress and the Pentagon are getting serious about this problem. It is now possible for victims to seek medical treatment without having to report the crime to police or their chain of command. More field hospitals have trained nurse practitioners to treat the victims; more bases have rape kits. "More than ever," Sanchez says, "I believe that our leadership at the very top is beginning to realize that they need to be proactive."

According to a report by the Defense Task Force on Sexual Assault in the Military Services, the progress made so far remains "evident, but uneven." The failure to provide a basic guarantee of safety to women, who now represent 15% of the armed forces, is not just a moral issue, or a morale issue. What does it say if the military can't or won't protect the people we ask to protect us? (by Nancy Gibbs)

MARRIAGE

Islam condemns adultery and encourages legal marriage. Celibacy is not considered as a sign of piety in Islam. Islam prescribes a very simple marriage process whereas puts barriers in the way of adultery.

We have already discussed in Chapter 6 that Islam gives a woman the right to choose her husband. There is a concept of 'Kafoo' in Islam according to which the equivalency of status of the girl and the boy should be considered at the time of match-making. Factors considered for this purpose includes family background, religion, piety, wealth, and profession. [19] But this rule can be ignored if the girl and her guardians agree, due to some reason, for the mismatch.

Marriages should not be unnessasarily delayed. Prophet Muhammad (P`BUH) said, "O Ali! Never postpone three things: 1) Namaz (prayer) when its time comes, 2) A funeral when it is ready, 3) The marriage of a women without husband, when suitable match is found for her." (Tirmizi)

Following is a brief discussion on the two wedding related topics mostly discussed by the opponents of Islam.

Polygamy:

Some people criticize Islam for allowing limited polygamy. Polygamy is of two types. One is polygyny where a man has more than one wife, and the other is polyandry, where a woman has more than one husband. Islam allows limited polygyny and prohibits polyandry completely. Islam permits a man to marry two, three or four women on the condition that he treats all of them justly. Prophet Muhammad (PBUH) said, "Whoso has two (or more) wives and does not treat them with equity and fairness, he will appear on the Day of Resurrection in such a condition that one side of his body would be fallen away." (Tirmizi, Abu Dawood, Nisai)

Some people have a misconception that it is necessary for a Muslim man to marry more than one woman. In Islam it is permissible but not compulsory and its legal status is that of 'Mubah' i.e permissible. In actual, very few men in a Muslim society are polygamist. According to a report in India, the percentage of polygamous marriages between the year 1951 -1961 was 5.06 among the Hindus and only 4.31 among the Muslims. [20]

In scriptures of other religions like the Vedas, the Ramayan, the Mahabharat, the Geeta or the Bible, one does not find any restriction on the number of wives a man can have at a time. However later on, Hindu priests and the Christian Church restricted the number of wives to one. Judaism permits Polygamy as well. Prophet Abraham (PBUH) had 2 wives and Prophet Solomon (PBUH) had hundreds of wives according to Talmudic law. The practice of polygamy continued in Judaism until Rabbi Gershom ben Yehudah (960 to 1030 A.D) issued an edict against it.

Men are biologically different from women and this is true in their sexual performance as well. Young men can have intercourse almost every day but women can't. A young woman experiences menstrual cycle for almost one week every month during which she is not available to her husband for intercourse. Her sexual capability diminishes during her nine months of pregnancy. After the birth of a child she suffers from lochia (postnatal bleeding) for two to six weeks. However during all those days a man remains sexually active. For some men with very intense sexual feelings, it would be very difficult to keep their patience during all these days. Hence if the second marriage is not allowed for them, there is a very high probability of their indulging in fornification.

The aging process of women is also faster than that of men. It may happen that a man remains potent till his late age and his wife becomes too old for him. In this case some percentage of such men can be inclined towards having illicit relationships with other younger women.

According to May 16, 2011 Fox News, 'On Sunday morning, the IMF chief and potential French presidential candidate was yanked off an Air France plane moments before departure and arrested on charges of a criminal sex act, attempted rape and unlawful imprisonment, police said. The IMF leader was accused of sexually assaulting a 32-year-old hotel maid, who told police that Strauss-Kahn attacked her when she entered his $3,000-a-night-suite to clean it on Saturday afternoon at the Sofitel Hotel near Times Square…Strauss-Kahn, the married father of four is known as DSK in France, but media there also have dubbed him "the great seducer." His reputation as a charmer of women has not hurt his career in France, where politicians' private lives traditionally come under less scrutiny than in the United States. In 2008, Strauss-Kahn was briefly investigated over whether he had an improper relationship with a subordinate female employee. The IMF board found that the relationship was consensual, but called his actions "regrettable" and said they "reflected a serious error of judgment."…A former economics professor, Strauss-Kahn joined the Socialist party in 1976 and was elected to parliament in 1986 from the Val-d'Oise district, north of Paris. He went on to become mayor of Sarcelles, a working-class immigrant suburb of Paris.'

If he was a great charmer of women and he was continuously failing to control his libido, then he should have become Muslim to solve his problem. Islam offers him a solution which many other systems fail to offer. Instead of using illegal means to fulfill his intense uncontrollable sexual desires, he would have four legal wives. This person is now surrounded with sex scandals that have destroyed his promising career. He ultimately resigned from the IMF.

A local television channel ran a sad story of a family. A man despite having one legal wife repeatedly raped his three daughters. His daughters had to undergo abortion many times. His eldest daughter even gave birth to a child. This man instead of repeatedly raping his three daughters could have three additional legal wives to satisfy his uncontrollable sexual desires. He was then behind bars and the whole family was suffering from the trauma.

Annie Besant (1847–1933) was a prominent British Theosophist, women's rights activist, writer and orator and supporter of Irish and Indian self rule. In her book 'The Life and Teachings of Muhammad' she wrote, "You will find others stating that the religion (Islam) is evil because it sanctions a limited polygamy. But you do not hear as a rule the criticism which I spoke out one day in a London hall where I knew that the audience was entirely uninstructed. I pointed out to them that monogamy with a blended mass of prostitution was hypocrisy and more degrading than a limited polygamy." [21]

Sometimes men have to pursue the option of second marriage in cases where their first wives are not capable of bearing the children. In this case this is also good for the first wife as she need not to be divorced before the second marriage.

Some other reasons regarding the permission of limited polygamy as given by famous Muslim scholar, Dr. Zakir Naik, are:

- *"Average life span of females is more than that of males. By nature males and females are born in approximately the same ratio. During paediatric age however, in childhood itself a female child has more immunity than a male child. A female child can fight the germs and diseases better than the male child. For this reason, there are more deaths among males as compared to the females during paediatric age. During wars, there are more men killed as compared to women. More men die due to accidents and diseases than women. The average life span of females is more than that of males, and at any given time one finds more widows in the world than widowers.*

- *World female population is more than male population. In the USA, women outnumber men by 7.8 million. New York alone has one million more females as compared to the number of males, and of the male population of New York one-third are gays i.e sodomites. The USA as a whole has more than twenty-five million gays. This means that these people do not wish to marry women. Great Britain has four million more females as compared to males. Germany has five million more females as compared to males. Russia has nine million more females than males. God alone knows how many million more females there are in the whole world as compared to males.*

- *Restricting each and every man to have only one wife is not practical. Even if every man got married to one woman, there would still be more than thirty million more females in USA who would not be able to get husbands (considering that America has twenty five million gays). There would be more than four million females in Great Britain 5 million females in Germany and nine million females in Russia alone who would not be able to find a husband. Suppose my sister happens to be one of the unmarried women living in USA, or suppose your sister happens to be one of the unmarried women in USA. The only two options remaining for her are that she either marries a man who already has a wife or becomes public property. There is no other option. I have posed this question to hundreds of non-Muslims and all opted for the first. However a few smart people before accepting, said they would prefer their sisters to remain virgins. Biologically, it is not possible for an average man or a woman to remain celibate throughout life. It may be possible in exceptional cases of one in ten thousand. In the vast majority, the person either gets married or performs illicit sex or indulges in other sexual perversions. Sex hormones are released in the adult body every day. That is the reason why Islam has prohibited Monasticism. In Western society it is common for a man to have mistresses and/or multiple extra-marital affairs, in which case, the woman leads a disgraceful, unprotected life. The same society, however, cannot accept a man having more than one wife, in which women retain their honourable, dignified position in society and lead a protected life. Islam prefers giving women the honourable position by permitting the first option and disallowing the second. There are several other reasons, why Islam has permitted limited polygyny, but it is mainly to protect the modesty of women."* [22] *(by Dr. Zakir Naik)*

From this discussion it is clear that the choice for us, therefore, is not between monogamy and polygamy, but rather, between the lawful polygamy or illicit polygamy. During the Second World War, in which several Western countries such as Germany, France, and Britain, took part, a large number of men were killed. As a result, women far outnumbered men at the end of hostilities. Permissiveness then became the order of the day, to the extent that boards with such inscription as 'Wanted - A guest for the evening' could be seen outside the homes of husbandless women. This state of affairs persisted in Western countries in various forms, even long after the war.

J.E Clare McFarlane (1894-1962) a poet and politician born in a Spanish town of Jamaica, writes in his book, "Whether the question is considered socially, ethically or religiously, it can be demonstrated that polygamy is not contrary to the highest standards of civilization…The suggestion offers a practical remedy for the problem of destitute and unwanted female; the alternative is continual and increased prostitution, concubinage and distressing spinsterhood." [23]

Early marriages:

Another favorite topic for condemnation of Islam is young marriages. A few years back someone raised an objection against Islam that it promotes early marriages for girls. My reply was stating some facts. According to Victor C. Strasburger, MD University of New Mexico School of Medicine:

- One million teens in the USA will become pregnant over the next twelve months. Ninety-five percent of those pregnancies are unintended. About one third will end in abortion; one third will end in spontaneous miscarriage; and one third will continue their pregnancy to term and keep their baby.
- More than half of them are 17 years old or younger when they have their first pregnancy.
- Approximately 40 percent of young women become pregnant before they reach 20 years old.
- The United States of America has double the adolescent pregnancy and birth rates of any other industrialized country.
- The poorer the young woman, the more likely she will become a mother.
- Less than one-third of teens who have babies before the age of 18 finish high school.
- Almost half of all teen mothers end up on welfare.
- Less than 25 percent of births to teens occur within wedlock. [24]

Was'nt marriage a better alternative for these girls? Islam does not force anyone for an early marriage. However marriage is considered a sunnat (practice of the Prophet Muhammad PBUH) and people are encouraged to marry without unnecessary delays. One can delay if there is some good reason for it.

Prophet Muhammad (PBUH) said, "O young people! Whoever among you can marry, should marry, because it helps him lower his gaze and guard his modesty, and whoever is not able to marry, should fast, as fasting diminishes his sexual power." (Bukhari)"

WOMEN WITNESS

The witness system according to Islamic jurisprudence is a bit complex to understand. I would therefore only briefly discuss some points here. There can be basically three types of witnesses by women:

Witness in matters that are mostly known by women only:

Examples of such matters are like child birth, virginity, and typical women issues. According to Islamic jurisprudence, in such matters, one woman's witness is enough and will be accepted. [25]

Financial and other miscellaneous matters:

Examples of such matters are debt, Nikah (marriage), divorce, will, and donations. According to Islamic jurisprudence, these types of matters require either two male witnesses or one male and two female witnesses. [26] Even one male witness is not enough.

According to the Holy Quran, "O you who believe, when you transact a debt payable at a specified time, put it in writing, and let a scribe write it between you with fairness. A scribe should not refuse to write as Allah has educated him. He, therefore, should write. The one who owes something should get it written, but he must fear Allah, his Lord, and he should not omit anything from it. If the one who owes is feeble-minded or weak or cannot dictate himself, then his guardian should dictate with fairness. Have two witnesses from among your men, and if two men are not there, then one man and two women from those witnesses whom you like, so that if one of the two women errs, the other woman may remind her...." (Surah Al-Baqarah, Chapter 2 Ayat 282)

This Quranic verse is regarding a financial matter in which Allah is commanding that we should have two males to witness such events. And if two males are not available then we should have one male and two females.

Generally speaking men all over the world are well-versed in financial and many other worldly matters as compared to women. Even in today's modern world we have seen a comparison of men and women in various matters including education. I have quoted UNDP in chapter 2 of this book according to which 'of the 960 million adults in the world who cannot read, two-thirds are women.' This is still a fact about women of our so called modern world. It is therefore natural that a man can be a better witness in such matters where they are generally well versed and have more exposure. Islam therefore being a natural religion is asking people to prefer two male witnesses in such matters. Even one male witness is not enough. And if two males are not available then we should have one male and two females as witnesses.

For Hudood and Qisas punishments:

These are the matters that require frequent visits to courts and interaction with other men. To provide witness in such matters is a very difficult process even for men.

Hudood is the plural of Hadd. These are those obligatory fixed punishments that are considered as right of Allah. The types of punishment for such limited number of crimes are set either directly in the Holy Quran or Hadith. These punishments are for 1) adultery/fornication, 2) false accusation of adultery/fornication, 3) apostasy, 4) having intoxicants, 5) theft, and 6) burglary. Qisaas-o-diyat system deals with various forms of murder and damages on body parts. As per the Islamic jurisprudence, in the case of adultery/fornification, four male witnesses are required. In other cases of Hudood and Qisaas, two male witnesses are enough. [27]

Tazeer is that discretionary correction which is administered for offences, for which Hadd or 'fixed punishment', has not been appointed. The head of the state or the legislative body can determine the punishments to be given in such cases. They have the right to set the punishments for such crimes depending upon factors like severity of crime, conditions under which the crime was committed, general atmosphere of the state, general behavior and attitude of the people, and so on. Depending upon such factors, the punishments can be light, severe or very severe. Normally Tazeer punishments are lighter than Hudood punishments but depending upon the severity of the crime, Tazeer punishments can even be equal to or more severe than Hudood punishments. Tazeer punishments are given in cases that are not covered by Hudood. These punishments are also given in cases that are covered by Hudood but the Hudood punishments cannot be administered due to reasons like lack of witnesses as per Hudood criteria.

Although a limited number of Hudood punishments require only male witnesses, the criminal can be given Tazeer punishment even if the male witnesses are not present and there are other signs that prove the crime. For example in the case that a crime takes place where only women are present. Their witness will also be considered by the court of justice to make some decision. In such case Hudood punishments will not be given but Tazeer punishments can be administered. And the type of Tazeer punishments will be determined by the court in the light of general guidance set by the state for administering such punishments. There are examples from the time of the companions of Prophet Muhammad (PBUH), when the decisions were taken solely based on women witnesses as the men were not present when the incident took place. For example, a man divorced his wife while he was intoxicated. Four women provided witness for this event. When this matter was brought to Caliph Umer (RAA), he allowed the testimony of women and separated the husband and wife. In another case a woman killed a child in front of other women where men were not present. Caliph Ali (RAA) settled the case based on the witness provided by four women and therefore blood money was asked from the criminal.

Providing witnesses – A privilege or a heavy responsibility:

It is clear from the preceding discussion that there are matters where only one female witness is enough, there are matters where male witnesses are preferred and there are a very limited number of Hudood / Qisas punishments where only male witnesses are required.

One should keep in mind that becoming a witness over some matter is an act of high responsibility. This point, however, can only be appreciated by a person who has himself or herself become a witness in a serious crime. I was once called by the anti-terrorist court in Pakistan to verify certain facts before the court of justice. The case was against a criminal involved in kidnapping and murder. The entire process was overwhelming and quite disturbing. I certainly would not want to be in such a situation again. This is the reason why most of the scholars say that Allah s.w.t has saved women from such matters that can prove to be troublesome or even harmful for her. The Islamic witness system may seem to be biased in favor of men but it saves women from a lot of trouble.

Being a witness in some matters can also become life threatening for example in murder trials, witnesses are under the constant threat of the criminals. Recently, in Karachi, five witnesses in a murder case of an influential television channel news reporter, were also systematically murdered. Just imagine if you were the sixth witness for this case. Even the prosecutor was murdered. This phenomenon is common all over the world. You can see Hollywood movies made exclusively on this subject, for example, in the movie 'Snakes in the plane', the murderers tried their level best to kill the male witness in a murder.

During a management training program at Lahore, one girl however explained the witness matter from a completely different angle. Her point was that being a girl she knows that there are certain times during a month when she is not in a position to effectively cope with the responsibility of providing witness in serious matters. What she was referring to was the women menstrual cycle. I did some research to evaluate her argument. My findings were that some uncomfortable side effects may be associated with a woman's menstrual cycle. These vary from woman to woman and from cycle to cycle. These may include cramping, heavy bleeding or nausea. Some women report that they are more emotional during their menstrual cycle and have a difficult time coping with their daily lives. Some girls and women cannot notice any pre-menstrual symptoms and can never feel the date of menstrual period. In general all pre-menstrual and menstrual symptoms mainly depend on hormones. Pre-menstrual symptoms called Premenstrual Syndrome (PMS) can be pretty disturbing. Depending on age and health status, the following psychological pre-menstrual symptoms are possible; aggression, anxiety, depression, difficulty in concentration, dizziness, headache, irritability, mood swings, troubled sleeping, troubles with concentrating and/or remembering. Besides pre-menstrual symptoms, the following symptoms could appear during menstruation; irritability, sadness, depression, emotional sensitivity, tiredness, "weepiness", tears of emotional closeness, psychotic episodes, rare menstruation may be a trigger (menstrual psychosis). [28]

INHERITANCE

Under Islamic law, why is a woman's share of the inherited wealth only half that of a man? Following is the answer to this question as given by world renouwned Islamic scholar, Dr. Zakir Naik:

"The Glorious Qur'an contains specific and detailed guidance regarding the division of the inherited wealth, among the rightful beneficiaries. The Qur'anic verses that contain guidance regarding inheritance are:

    * Surah Baqarah, Chapter 2 Verse 180
    * Surah Baqarah, Chapter 2 Verse 240
    * Surah Nisa, Chapter 4 Verse 7-9
    * Surah Nisa, Chapter 4 Verse 19
    * Surah Nisa, Chapter 4 Verse 33 and
    * Surah Maidah, Chapter 5 Verse 106-108

There are three verses in the Qur'an that broadly describe the share of close relatives i.e. Surah Nisah Chapter 4 Verses 11, 12 and 176. The translations of these verses are as follows:

"Allah (swt) (thus) directs you as regards your children's (inheritance): to the male, a portion equal to that of two females, if only daughters, two or more, their share is two-thirds of the inheritance; If only one, her share is a half.

For parents, a sixth share of the inheritance to each, if the deceased left children; If no children, and the parents are the (only) heirs, the mother has a third; if the deceased left brothers (or sisters) the mother has a sixth. (The distribution in all cases is) after the payment of legacies and debts. Ye know not whether your parents or your children are nearest to you in benefit. These are settled portions ordained by Allah; and Allah is All-Knowing, All-Wise.

In what your wives leave, your share is half. If they leave no child; but if they leave a child, ye get a fourth; after payment of legacies and debts. In what ye leave, their share is a fourth, if ye leave no child; but if ye leave a child, they get an eight; after payment of legacies and debts. If the man or woman whose inheritance is in question, has left neither ascendants nor descendants, but has left a brother or a sister, each one of the two gets a sixth; but if more than two, they share in a third; after payment of legacies and debts; so that no loss is caused (to anyone). Thus it is ordained by Allah; and Allah is All-Knowing Most Forbearing" [Al-Qur'an 4:11-12]

"They ask thee for a legal decision. Say: Allah directs (them) about those who leave no descendants or ascendants as heirs. If it is a man that dies, leaving a sister but no child, she shall have half the inheritance. If (such a deceased was) a woman who left no child, Her brother takes her inheritance. If there are two sisters, they shall have two thirds of the inheritance (between them). If there are brothers and sisters, (they share), the male having twice the share of the female. Thus doth Allah (swt) makes clear to you (His knowledge of all things)." [Al-Qur'an 4:176]

In most of the cases, a woman inherits half of what her male counterpart inherits. However, this is not always the case. In case the deceased has left no ascendant or descendent but has left the uterine brother and sister, each of the two inherit one sixth. If the deceased has left children, both the parents that is mother and father get an equal share and inherit one sixth each. In certain cases, a woman can also inherit a share that is double that of the male. If the deceased is a woman who has left no children, brothers or sisters and is survived only by her husband, mother and father, the husband inherits half the property while the mother inherits one third and the father the remaining one sixth. In this particular case, the mother inherits a share that is double that of the father. It is true that as a general rule, in most cases, the female inherits a share that is half that of the male. For instance in the following cases:

1. Daughter inherits half of what the son inherits,
2. Wife inherits 1/8th and husband 1/4th if the deceased has no children.
3. Wife inherits 1/4th and husband 1/2 if the deceased has children
4. If the deceased has no ascendant or descendent, the sister inherits a share that is half that of the brother.

In Islam a woman has no financial obligation and the economical responsibility lies on the shoulders of the man. Before a woman is married it is the duty of the father or brother to look after the lodging, boarding, clothing and other financial requirements of the woman. After she is married it is the duty of the husband or the son. Islam holds the man financially responsible for fulfilling the needs of his family. In order to do be able to fulfill the responsibility the men get double the share of the inheritance. For example, if a man dies leaving about Rs. One Hundred and Fifty Thousand, for the children (i.e one son and one daughter) the son inherits One Hundred Thousand rupees and the daughter only Fifty Thousand rupees. Out of the one hundred thousand which the son inherits, as his duty towards his family, he may have to spend on them almost the entire amount or say about eighty thousand and thus he has a small percentage of inheritance, say about twenty thousand, left for himself. On the other hand, the daughter, who inherits fifty thousand is not bound to spend a single penny on anybody. She can keep the entire amount for herself. Would you prefer inheriting one hundred thousand rupees and spending eighty thousand from it, or inheriting fifty thousand rupees and having the entire amount to yourself? [29] (by Dr. Zakir Naik)

SOME OTHER AREAS OF DIFFERENTIATION:

In Chapter 4 we identified some essential differences between men and women that cannot be denied. In chapter 6, we discussed that scientifically it is wrong to say that these differences are due to 'Social Construct' only. There are many differences due to factors developed in a baby when he or she is in her mother's womb. It is a scientific fact that the two sexes are different. It is therefore wrong to treat them alike, in each and every respect.

As quoted before, according to a lady, Eva Evelyn Burrows, "We have to be careful in this era of radical feminism, not to emphasize an equality of the sexes that leads women to imitate men to prove their equality. To be equal does not mean you have to be the same." [30] And even those societies that ignored this fact, failed to bring perfect equality of treatment of the two sexes. As quoted before, Russian Scientist Anton Nemilov, explains, "Very few people will agree if it is said today that women should be given limited rights in the social setup. We, too, are wholly against such a suggestion. However, we should not deceive ourselves in thinking that establishing equality between men and women in practical life is a simple matter. Nowhere have more attempts been made than in the USSR to establish this equality. Nowhere in the world have such unbiased and generous laws been made than in the USSR, yet it is a fact that the position of woman in a family has hardly changed for the better." [31]

Islam being a natural religion also does differentiate in certain matters between men and women. Despite the fact that Islam gives full respect and honour to both the sexes, some of the Islamic teachings vary between men and women. This is evident from the previous discussions in this chapter. However matters like these are quoted by the opponents of Islam to give a false impression that Islam oppresses women. There are areas in which Islam in fact seems to favour women. These matters, however, are either entirely not quoted or are distorted to give a false impression about Islam. Following is a list of some such matters:

- There are many relaxations given to women in various Islamic worships that are not given to men. For example, it is emphasized that men should pray their daily five prayers in a congregation in the mosque while it is not emphasized upon women who can pray easily at their homes. Men have to wear unstitched clothes during the Hajj as ihram (that is difficult to handle) while women wear stitched clothes.

- Islam frees women from the burden of earning the livelihood. It is the responsibility of the husband or other male members to provide for the family.

- Not only has Islam exempted the women from any financial responsibility for earning for herself and her family, Islam has also given her the free will to spend her money in whatever way she wants too. This money could be in the form of her own earning, or her inheritance, or the pocket money she gets from her husband. Man on the other hand, does not have this kind of freedom. He has been bound to provide for his family. (Here I would like to clarify that a woman has certain religious financial obligations, for example, just like a man she also has to pay Zakat on her wealth. However her husband or any other man can help her in fulfilling these financial obligations.)

- In Islam wearing silk or gold is entirely forbidden for men whereas women can use these things. Prophet Muhammad (PBUH) said, "Wearing silk and gold has been made unlawful for the males of my Ummah and lawful for their females." (Tirmidhi)

- Islam frees women from the heavy burden of physically fighting with the enemy in case of a war. Men fight in the wars and risk their lives. This is a heavy responsibility on men for which women have been exempted.

- Earning paradise is also comparatively easy for women. Prophet Muhammad (PBUH) said, "The woman who offers her prayers regularly, fasts in the month of Ramazan, preserves her chastity and obeys her husband, will be asked (after her death) to enter the Paradise through whichever gate she likes." (Ahmed, Tibrani)

- Earning paradise is also comparatively easy for a man who has daughters. Prophet Muhammad (PBUH) said, "The one upon whom the trying responsibility of (raising) daughters was placed and he (or she) fulfilled this responsibility in a good manner treating them well, for him (or her) these daughters shall become the means of protection from Hell." (Sahih Bukhari, Sahih Muslim)

- In Islam, a woman does not have to display her body to earn success. In many cultures her body is very much exposed as compared to that of men. We usually see men wearing suits, ties, etc, and women wearing skin tight clothes, mini skirts, sleeveless shirts, etc. In the Islamic culture, their bodies are covered more than that of men. Thus Islam does not want to 'objectify' women.

- Islam puts no financial burden on a woman and her family at the time of her wedding whereas it does put some financial responsibility on the bridegroom like giving dower to the bride and arranging Valima ceremony.

- As discussed in Chapter 6, Islam gives more respect to various feminine roles in a society as compared to that of males. For example, it gives more respect to a mother than to a father. A mother is three times more eligible for good treatment by her children as compared to a father. A man came to Prophet Muhammad (PBUH) and said, "O Allah's Apostle! Who is more entitled to be treated with the best companionship by me?" The Prophet said, "Your mother." The man said. "Who is next?" The Prophet said, "Your mother." The man further said, "Who is next?" The Prophet said, "Your mother." The man asked for the fourth time, "Who is next?" The Prophet said, "Your father." (Sahih Bukhari)

Some other favours of Islam on women are:

- In Islam, a woman does not have to assume the husband name as if she is her husband's property. In the 1860s, a married Englishwoman did not exist as a legal person. Upon marriage she entered a condition called 'converture', effectively making her a possession of her husband. Her name was changed to indicate the new ownership, a practice that continues to date even in developed countries.

- Islam liberates a woman from the modern tyranny of having to become a man in order to get a sense of self worth and achievement. In Islam, while being fully feminine, she gets full respect and honor. Islam does not allow a woman to resemble a man and vice-versa. Prophet Muhammad (PBUH) said, "Allah curses men who adopt resemblance of women and women who adopt resemblance of men." (Bukhari)

- Islam frees women from the anti-women concepts of some religions. For example, Christianity has the concept of 'Original Sin' which puts full responsibility of eating the fruit of the forbidden tree in heaven on woman. According to the Bible, "When the woman (Eve) saw that the fruit of the tree was good for food and pleasing to eye, and also desirable for gaining wisdom, she took some and ate it. She also gave some to her husband (Adam), ...". The Bible also mentions that God said to the women, "I will greatly increase your pains in childbearing; with pain you will give birth to children. Your desire will be for your husband, and he will rule over you." As mentioned in Bible, God said to Adam (AS), "Because you listen to your wife and ate from the tree about which I commanded you, 'You must not eat of it', cursed is the ground because of you, through painful toil you will eat of it all the days of your life." (Genesis 3: 6-17)

The Islamic concept of this incident is very different from the concept in Christianity. According to the Holy Quran, both Adam AS and Eve AS were deceived by Satan. Secondly, contrary to the biblical version, according to the Holy Quran, God forgave both Adam AS and Eve AS before sending them to this world, where they were originally meant to go. Their stay in paradise was temporary before moving them to earth as the vicegerent of God. During their stay in paradise, it was demonstrated to them that Satan is their real enemy and they should be in future careful of his deceptions. They were not sent to the earth as punishment. These points are clear from the following sentences in Holy Quran:

"(Remember) when your Lord said to the angels, 'I am going to create a deputy on the earth!' They said, 'Will You create there one who will spread disorder on the earth and cause bloodshed, while we proclaim Your purity, along with your praise, and sanctify Your name?'. He said, 'Certainly, I know what you know not.' And He taught Adam the names, all of them; then presented them before the angels, and said, 'Tell me their names, if you are right.' They said, 'To You belongs all purity! We have no knowledge except what You have given us. Surely, You alone are the All-knowing, All-wise.' He said, 'O Adam, tell them the names of all these.' When he told them their names, Allah said, 'Did I not tell you that I know the secrets of the skies and of the earth, and that I know what you disclose and what you conceal.' And when We said to the angels: 'Prostrate yourselves before Adam!' So, they prostrated themselves, all but Iblis (Satan). He refused, and became one of the infidels. And We said, 'O Adam, dwell, you and your wife, in Paradise; and eat at pleasure wherever you like, but do not go near this tree, otherwise you will be (counted) among the transgressors.' Then, Satan caused them to slip from it, and brought them out of where they had been. And We said, 'Go down, all of you, some of you the enemies of others; and on the earth there will be for you a dwelling place and enjoyment for a time.' Then Adam learned certain words (to pray with) from his Lord; so, Allah accepted his repentance. No doubt, He is the Most-Relenting, the Very-Merciful. We said, 'Go down from here, all of you. Then, should some guidance come to you from Me, those who follow My guidance shall have no fear, nor shall they grieve. As for those who disbelieve, and deny Our signs, they are the people of the Fire. They shall dwell in it forever.'" (Surah Baqarah, Ayats 30 – 39)

As mentioned, according to the Bible, God said to the women, "I will greatly increase your pains in childbearing; with pain you will give birth to children……" Therefore whatever painful experiences a woman suffers during child birth, according to Bible, is a form of punishment. On the contrary, according to the Holy

Qur'an, pregnancy and child birth have uplifted the women, not degraded her. According to the Holy Quran, "We commanded man (to be good) in respect of his parents. His mother carried him (in her womb) despite weakness upon weakness, and his weaning is in two years. (We said to man,) Be grateful to Me, and to your parents. To Me is the ultimate return." (Surah Luqman, Ayat 14)

At the end of this book, I will give another example to appreciate the kind of respect and importance Islam gives to women. The rite of sa'i, is an important part of the pilgrimage of Mecca (Hajj), made at least once in a lifetime as a religious duty by all Muslims who can afford the journey. The rite of sa'i is performed by walking back and forth seven times between Safa and Marwah, two hillocks near the Holy Kabah. This walking enjoined upon every pilgrim, be man or woman, be they rich or poor, literate or illiterate, Kings or commoners, is in imitation of the desperate quest of Bibi Hagara AS (Hagar), the wife of Hazrat Ibrahim's AS (Abraham), for water to quench the thirst of her crying infant when they arrived in the dry desert country, thousands of years ago in the city of Mecca. Perhaps there could be no better demonstration of a woman's greatness than God's command to men, literally to follow in her foot-steps during this rite.

A few days back I received the following email from a women wing of an UK based Islamic organization denouncing a call of some feminists:

"Have you heard about the new wave of feminists seeking to liberate women from the shackles of Islam by telling us to take part in a topless jihad? What do they want to free us from?

Is it our Dignity they want to free us from?

The fact that our creator didn't just want us to be treated as mere sex-objects but protected us by commanding us to cover ourselves? That He made us sacred, so that if a man wants to be close to us he has to commit to us? Nudity only objectifies women further - when confronted with a topless woman, the last thing men are thinking about is how much they respect their cause and intelligence!

Is it our History they want to free us from?

The fact that a thousand years before women in Europe were allowed into University, Muslim women such as Fatima al-Fihri were founding Universities? That we were given the right to inheritance, to property, to political participation, to be spiritual equals to men over a thousand years before women in Europe were? Is that what they want to liberate us from?

Is it our Creator they want to free us from?

Who knows us better than we know ourselves, who taught us to live not according to the whims and desires and subjective views of men whose moral lens keeps changing, but according to timeless moral principles that protect our interests and the interests of society?

Is it our Messenger they want to free us from?

Who (peace be upon him) said: "The Best of you is the one who is the best to wife" and gave us as mothers three times more rights than fathers?

If that is the case then they can keep their version of freedom. I am a slave - not to societal constructs, not to the subjective ideas of man, not to the morality of a materialistic society, but to Allah - my Creator.

What we need is a Jihad against ignorance. You, my sister have AISHA as a role model, KHADIJAH as a grandmother, ASMAA' as a sister... never forget who you are." [32] Islam is a beautiful and fair religion to all the men and women. The anti-Islamic false claims regarding unjust treatment of women by Islam are only weak attempts to make the true religion look bad. The truth of Islam will always prevail.

Appendices

Appendix A:

How to become a Muslim?

"Whoever seeks a faith other than Islam, it will never be accepted from him, and he, in the Hereafter, will be among the losers." *(Holy Quran, Surah Al Imran, Chapter 3, Ayat 85)*

The word "Muslim" means one who submits to the will of God, regardless of their race, nationality or ethnic background. Becoming a Muslim is a simple and easy process. One may convert alone in privacy, or he/she may do so in the presence of others. If anyone wants to become a Muslim then, all one needs to do is pronounce the "Shahada" (the testimony of faith) without further delay. The Holy Quran and prophetic sayings both stress the importance of following Islam.

According to the Holy Quran, "The Religion before Allah is Islam (submission to His will)..." (Surah Al Imran, Chapter 3, Ayat 19)

Prophet Muhammad (PBUH) said, "If anyone testifies that none has the right to be worshipped but Allah Alone Who has no partners, and that Muhammad is His Slave and His Apostle, and that Jesus is Allah's Slave and His Apostle and His Word which He bestowed on Mary and a Spirit created by Him, and that Paradise is true, and Hell is true, Allah will admit him into Paradise with the deeds which he had done even if those deeds were few." (Junada, the sub-narrator said, " 'Ubada added, 'Such a person can enter Paradise through any of its eight gates he likes.' ") (Sahih Bukhari) This Hadith confirms that all Prophets of Allah were human beings and thus refutes those who attribute divinity to them and exclude them from the category of men or regard them a part of God.

To become a Muslim one must simply pronounce the Shahada with sincerity and conviction. The Shahada can be declared as: "ASH-HADU ALLA-ELA-HA IL-LALLA-HU WAH-DAHU LA-SHAREEKA-LAHU. WA ASH-HADU ANNA MOHAMMADAN AB-DOHU WA-RASOO-LAHU. These words are in Arabic. The translation is: "I bear witness that there is no god but Allah, the only one, He has no partners. And I bear witness that Muhammad is His servant and His messenger."

The person who wants to become a Muslim should preferably perform ablution (Wuzoo) or take a bath (Ghusal) before reciting the Shahada. To become a Muslim one can recite the Shahada in front of any Muslim. If one does not get a chance of ablution or a bath and recites the Shahada even then he or she will be considered as a Muslim. If he or she will declare his Islam to other Muslims then they will accept this declaration.

If a person becomes a Muslim and he or she was unclean due to any reason for example having sexual relation or after menstrual cycle, and if in such a condition he or she has not taken a bath or if he or she has taken a bath but the bath was not complete as per Islamic instructions then it is necessary for him or her to have a proper bath in the Islamic way after accepting Islam.

If someone is clean before accepting Islam then taking a new bath before reciting Shahada is not necessary but is considered as a good practice. If someone wants to take a bath then following are some of its basics:

In Islam there is a prescribed method for taking a bath however if a person takes a normal bath for example takes a shower and has performed the following three activities during the bath then his or her Ghusal (Islamic way of bath) will be valid. These are the obligatory actions required for a Ghusal:

Water has reached all the body parts including the hair leaving no part dry.

One has thoroughly rinsed the mouth with water.

Water is taken inside the nostrils to clean the nose from inside till the soft part of the nose.

Some other advice are; Before starting to wash, one should be sure that he or she has concealed himself from others. Place the clothes and towel in a clean place. When using soap, this must be followed by clean water so that none of the soap remains on the body. This is required when washing is obligatory. Bathing in a bath tub is permitted, provided that one follows this by taking a shower to guarantee that all impurities have been removed.

When someone pronounces the testimony (Shahada) with conviction, then he or she has become a Muslim. It can be done alone, but it is much better to be done with the help of a Muslim so that he or she may help you in pronouncing the Shahada and to provide you with important resources for the new Muslims.

When people accept Islam, they in essence repent from the ways and beliefs of their previous life. One need not be overburdened by sins committed before their acceptance. After accepting Islam a person's record is cleaned, and it is as if he or she was just born from his mother's womb. According to the Holy Quran, "And those who believed and did righteous deeds and believed in that which is revealed to Muhammad, and it is the truth (that has come) from their Lord, He will write off their evil deeds, and will set aright their state of affairs." (Surah Muhammad, Chapter 47, Ayat 2) One should however try as much as possible to keep his or her records clean and strive to do as many good deeds as possible in the future.

What would be next after declaring oneself a Muslim? One should then know the real concept underlying the testimony which means the

Oneness of Allah and meet its requirements. One must behave accordingly, applying this true faith to every thing one speaks or does. We have to consider that when we declare from our heart that there is no god but Allah, it implies on our part love, devotion, faith and obedience to the rules of Islamic legislations which are legally binding on all Muslims.

If you are a non-Muslim, I invite you towards Islam. Allah states in the Holy Quran, "Let there be no compulsion in religion. Truth stands out clear from error; whoever rejects evil and believes in Allah, hath grasped the most trustworthy hand-hold that never breaks. And Allah heareth and knoweth all things." (Surah Baqarah, Chapter 2, Ayat 256).

But one must be careful. Unfortunately today one can find many groups and sects claiming to be the best Muslims. However not all of them are exactly on the right path. Some among them are deviated sects while others are even out of the folds of Islam. For example Qadyanis or Ahmadis do not consider Prophet Muhammad (PBUH) as the last Prophet from God. They believe in the false prophethood of another person therefore they are out of the folds of Islam. One should be careful not to follow such groups or deviated sects. You can also contact us at the e-mail address adeelzeerak@hotmail.com for any guidance in this matter.

Appendix B:

Introduction to a book on Islam

Readers who want to discover more about Islam can read the book, ISLAM: A SUPERIOR SYSTEM OF LIFE by the same author Adeel Zeerak. Following are the salient features of the book:

ISLAM: A SUPERIOR SYSTEM OF LIFE

ISBN: 1-4775-1710-3

ISBN-13: 978-1-4775-1710-9

One of the largest and fastest-growing religions, Islam is currently practiced by approximately one-fifth of the world's population. Unlike most religions that only consist of acts of worship, rituals, and a set of beliefs, it also offers a just socio-politico-economic system, which is especially important today as we continue to make significant material and scientific progress. However, although it presents real solutions to problems faced by the whole of mankind, factors such as worldwide media propaganda and the current condition of the Muslim community have seriously distorted the public image of Islam. Adeel Zeerak hopes that his book Islam: A Superior System of Life will help change all that.

He says that after careful study, even those with non-Muslim unprejudiced minds will appreciate the beauty of his religion's teachings. To prove the superiority of Islamic system over other systems, he provides concrete data obtained from authentic sources and refrains from using boastful or exaggerative language. Chapters in Islam: A Superior System of Life includes:

1. This is Islam
2. Characteristics of the Islamic System
3. Spiritual System
4. Social System
5. Economic System
6. Political System
7. The Prophet, peace be upon him, the Message, and the Ummah

"Despite commendable progress in the field of science and technology, this world is full of evil, exploitation, and injustice," says Zeerak, who believes any effort to find a solution to our problems continually fails because we choose to ignore the light of Divine Guidance. We all know what happened to prophet Noah's people when they rejected this guidance, but we, thankfully, still exist in this world to follow our Lord and accept Islam.

Written for the Muslim and non-Muslim, Islam: A Superior System of Life is for readers interested in Islam, the prophet Muhammad (PBUH), the Islamic view of women, the concept of Khilafat, Islamic finance, Islamic spirituality, and Islamic history. The author promises that our obedience to Allah, subhanahu wa-ta'ala, will result in endless favors and blessings both in this world and the hereafter.

"The book's greatest success is that it presents Islam as a dynamic, adaptive, and ultimately humanitarian, faith that has something to offer followers in every aspect of their daily lives. In this way, it amends much of the false and reductive rhetoric that has been applied to the faith in the wake of 9/11."

KIRKUS INDIE REVIEW

Notes

Dedication

1 This is according to the Muslim belief. Prophet Muhammad (PBUH) said, "Look after your mother because your Heaven lies beneath her feet".

Acknowledgement

1 s.w.t stands for 'Subhanahu wa-ta'ala'. It is an Arabic phrase that can be translated in English as: 'glorified and exalted be He' or 'may He be glorified and exalted' or 'he is glorified and exalted'. The phrase appears after the name of God in Islamic texts. Saying this phrase is seen as an act of reverence and devotion towards God among Muslims.

Chapter 1: Women are women

1 This information was taken from the internet website link: http://psychology.about.com/od/sigmundfreud

2 This information was taken from the internet website link: http://www.cbsnews.com/8301-205_162-57353346/stephen-hawkings-biggest-mystery-at-70-women/

3 This organization was ActionAid

4 This article was published on September 16, 2012. It was taken from the internet website link: http://www.psychologytoday.com/blog/21st-century-aging/201209/differences-between-men-and-women

5 PBUH stands for 'Peace be upon him'. This is a phrase that practising Muslims often say after saying (or hearing) the name of one of the Prophets of Islam.

Chapter 2: Problems faced by women

1 United Nations Development Programme (UNDP) and Government of Sindh (Pakistan), Gender Sensitive Project Planning Skills Training, 2010.

2 This information is taken from the internet website like: http://www.un.org/en/pseataskforce/overview.shtml

3 "The revolution", Dawn (Pakistan), 9 December 2012.

4 This information is taken from the internet website: www.feminist.com

5 "The revolution", Dawn (Pakistan), 9 December 2012.

6 This information is taken from the internet website: www.feminist.com

7 Ibid

8 This information is taken from the internet website link: http://www.unodc.org/southeastasiaandpacific/en/topics/illicit-trafficking/human-trafficking-definition.html

9 This information is taken from the internet website link: http://www.state.gov/j/tip/rls/tiprpt/2005/46606.htm

10 Catherine A. MacKinnon, <u>Are Women Human?</u>, (Belknap Press of Harvard University Press, 2007).

11 This information is taken from the internet website: www.feminist.com

12 William B. Werther, Jr. and Keith Davis, <u>Human Resources and Personnel Management</u>, 5th edition (McGraw-Hill Inc., 1996), p. 398.

13 Patrice C. McMahon, "The effect of political and economic reforms on Soviet/Russian women", <u>Women in the age of economic transformation: gender impact of reforms in post-socialist and developing countries</u>, (1994).

14 William B. Werther, Jr. and Keith Davis, <u>Human Resources and Personnel Management</u>, 5th edition (McGraw-Hill Inc., 1996), p. 89.

15 This information is taken from the internet website: www.feminist.com

16 Dr. Henry Makow, "The Debauchery of American Womanhood". I have downloaded this article from the internet website link: http://www.islamreligion.com/articles/532/

17 Patrice C. McMahon, "The effect of political and economic reforms on Soviet/Russian women", <u>Women in the age of economic transformation: gender impact of reforms in post-socialist and developing countries</u>, (1994).

18 Debora Spar, "Why Women Should Stop Trying to Be Perfect". I have downloaded this article from the internet website link: http://www.thedailybeast.com/newsweek/2012/09/23/why-women-should-stop-trying-to-be-perfect.html

19 This information is taken from the internet website: www.feminist.com

20 Ibid

Chapter 3: What is Feminism?

1 This quote is taken from the internet website: thinkexist.com.

2 Please note that not all but a lot of information in this chapther regarding Feminism is taken from Wikipedia.

3 Dr. Henry Makow, "The Debauchery of American Womanhood". I have downloaded this article from the internet website link: http://www.islamreligion.com/articles/532/

4 Information taken from the article: Yvonne Ridley, "How I Came to Love the Veil". This article is available at the internet website link: http://yvonneridley.org/2006/how-i-came-to-love-the-veil

Chapter 4: Equity or Equality

1 This quote is taken from the internet website: thinkexist.com.

2 This article was published on September 16, 2012. It was taken from the internet website link: http://www.psychologytoday.com/blog/21st-century-aging/201209/differences-between-men-and-women

3 Nancy Shute, "His brain, her brain", U.S. News & World Report, 2005.

4 Ibid

5 This article was published on March 19, 2007. It was taken from the internet website link: http://www.steadyhealth.com/articles/Difference_Between_Male_And_Female_Structures__Mental_And_Physical__a613.html?show_all=1

6 I have purposely not mentioned the name and exact location of this plant.

7 This information is taken from the internet website link: http://www.unicef.org/mdg/files/Overarching_2Pager_Web.pdf

8 United Nations Development Programme (UNDP) and Government of Sindh (Pakistan), Gender Sensitive Project Planning Skills Training, 2010.

9 This article was published on September 16, 2012. It was taken from the internet website link: http://www.psychologytoday.com/blog/21st-century-aging/201209/differences-between-men-and-women

10 Dr. Henry Makow, "The Debauchery of American Womanhood". I have downloaded this article from the internet website link: http://www.islamreligion.com/articles/532/

11 This article is taken from the internet website link: http://laradavid.blogspot.com/2008/07/difference-between-equity-and-equality.html

Chapter 5: Liberation or Debauchery

1 Khalid Baig, "Gold and glitter". I have downloaded this article from the internet website link: http://www.albalagh.net/women/gold_and_glitter.shtml

2 Yvonne Ridley, "How I Came to Love the Veil". This article is available at the internet website link: http://yvonneridley.org/2006/how-i-came-to-love-the-veil

3 Aftab Ahmed Shamsi, Islam ko chupao warna baghawat phel jai gee, (Lahore: Pakistan Islamic Center, 1984), p. 81 – 82.

4 Dr. Henry Makow, "The Debauchery of American Womanhood". I have downloaded this article from the internet website link: http://www.islamreligion.com/articles/532/

5 Strasburger, V. C., University of New Mexico School of Medicine, Teen Pregnancy Rates in the USA, 2004. I have found this information at the internet website: http://www.aishtamid.org/pdfs/teen/TeenPregnancyRates.pdf

6 Fiona Macrae, "Shocking figures show teenagers have a quarter of abortions in Britain", daily Mail (UK), 30 December 2011.

7 This information is taken from the internet website link: http://www.hhs.gov/ash/oah/adolescent-health-topics/reproductive-health/teen-pregnancy/

8 Alan J. Hawkins and Tamara A. Fackrell, Should I keep trying to work it out?, (Utah: 2009), p. 41.

9 Ibid

10 Ibid, P. 43

11 Ibid

12 Ibid

13 This information is taken from the internet website: www.Wikipedia.com

14 "Children in single parent families 'worse behaved'", Telegraph (UK). This information is taken from the internet website link: http://www.telegraph.co.uk/education/educationnews/8064435/Children-in-single-parent-families-worse-behaved.html

15 Donna M. Hughes, "Men Create the Demand; Women Are the Supply", November 2000. This information has been taken from the internet website link: http://www.uri.edu/artsci/wms/hughes/demand.htm.

16 This information is taken from the internet website: www.thinkexist.com

Chapter 6: Islam and women

1 This hadith is mentioned in the book, Abu Dawood.

2 Dr. Mufti Abdul Wahid, Masail-i-Bihishti Zewar vol. 1, (Karachi: Majlis-i-Nasharyat-i-Islam, 2007), p. 30 - 31.

3 G. A. Parwez, "Genesis and ideology of Pakistan".

4 Mufti Muhammad Taqi Usmani, An introduction to Islamic Finance, (Karachi: Maktaba Ma'ariful Quran, 2002), p. 15 – 16.

5 These quotations are taken from the internet website: thinkexist.com.

6 Michael Moore, "Capitalism: A Love Story", September 2009.

7 These quotations are taken from the internet website: thinkexist.com.

8 Michael Hart, The 100: A ranking of the most influential persons in history, (Great Britain: Simon & Schuster Ltd, 1992), p. 330.

9 Sarojini Naidu, The Ideals of Islam vide Speeches and Writings of Sarojini Naidu, (Madrass: 1918), p. 167.

10 Napolean Bonaparte as quoted in Christian Cherfils, Bonaparte et Islam, Pedone Ed., (Paris: 1914).

11 Adeel Zeerak, <u>Islam: A Superior System of Life</u>, (USA: Createspace, 2012). This book is available at www.Amazon.com.

12 Yvonne Ridley, "How I Came to Love the Veil". This article is available at the internet website link: http://yvonneridley.org/2006/how-i-came-to-love-the-veil

13 Annie Besant, <u>The Life and Teachings of Muhammad</u>, (Madras: June 1932), p. 25 – 26.

14 I have downloaded this article from the internet website link: http://www.albalagh.net/education/002.shtml

15 Dr. Mufti Abdul Wahid, <u>Masail-i-Bihishti Zewar vol. 2</u>, (Karachi: Majlis-i-Nasharyat-i-Islam, 2007), p. 43.

16 Annie Besant, <u>The Life and Teachings of Muhammad</u>, (Madras: June 1932), p. 3.

17 Michael Hart, <u>The 100: A ranking of the most influential persons in history</u>, (Great Britain: Simon & Schuster Ltd, 1992), p. 265.

18 Syeda Akefah Hashmi, "Women's Education in Islam", <u>The Intellect</u>, December–January, 2012-13, p. 32.

19 Speech at Jinnah Islamia College for Girls, Lahore, 22 November 1942.

20 Callie Marie Rennison, U.S. Dep't of Just., NCJ 197838, Bureau of Justice Statistics Crime Data Brief: Intimate Partner Violence, 1993-2001.

21 This information is taken from the internet website: www.feminist.com

22 Patrice C. McMahon, "The effect of political and economic reforms on Soviet/Russian women", <u>Women in the age of economic transformation: gender impact of reforms in post-socialist and developing countries</u>, (1994).

23 Philip Cohen, "America is still a Patriarchy". This article is available at the internet website link: http://www.theatlantic.com/sexes/ archive/2012/11/america-is-still-a-patriarchy/265428/inShare

24 Professor Steven Golberg, The Inevitability of Patriarchy. This information is taken from internet website link: http://news.google.com/ newspapers?nid=1946&dat=19770715&id=dpcuAAAAIBAJ&sjid=iaE FAAAAIBAJ&pg=1315,3114128

25 Allan Mazur and Alan Booth, "Testosterone and Dominance in Men". This information is taken from the internet website link: http:// cogprints.org/663/1/bbs_mazur.html

26 "Programed By Fetal Testosterone, Study Finds", Live Science, June 2012. This information is taken from the internet website link: http://www.huffingtonpost.com/2012/11/06/boys-behavior-fetal-testosterone_n_2082720.html

27 Please refer to the full article in chapter 4.

28 Anton Nemilov, The Biological Tragedy of Women, (London: 1932), p. 76.

29 This information is taken from the internet website: www.feminist.com.

30 Dr. Muhammad Iqbal, The Reconstruction of Religious Thought in Islam. Text of this book consisting of Dr. Iqbal's lectures is available at the internet website link: http://www.allamaiqbal.com/works/prose/ english/reconstruction/06.htm

31 Women Commission Jamat-i-Islami Pakistan, "Pakistan key mukhtalif soobon main raij ghalat rasoomat aur un key nuqsanat".

32 This information is taken from the internet website: http:// www.irf.net/index.php?option=com_content&view=article&id= 386%3Avast-difference-between-islam-and-the-actual-practice-of-

muslims&catid=71%3Amost-common-questions-asked-by-non-muslim&Itemid=199.

Chapter 7: Is Islam against women?

1 "Why British Women are turning to Islam", The Times, 9 November 1993.

2 Dr. Malik Ghulam Murtaza, Socio-Economic System of Islam, (Lahore: Seerat Enterprises), p. 231 – 232.

3 I was myself part of this training held at Pakistan Institute of Management, Karachi, Pakistan.

4 Michael P. Todaro, Economic Development, 6th edition (Addison Wesley Longman, 1996), p. 235.

5 Dr. Henry Makow, "The Debauchery of American Womanhood". I have downloaded this article from the internet website link: http://www.islamreligion.com/articles/532/

6 "The world is changing". Youtube link to this video is: http://www.youtube.com/watch?v=EKYdO193eoc

7 Annie Besant, The Life and Teachings of Muhammad, (Madras: June 1932), p. 25 – 26.

8 Khalid Baid, "Home, Sweet Home". I have downloaded this article from the internet website link: http://www.albalagh.net/women/gold_and_glitter.shtml

9 Nicholas D. Kristof and Sheryl Wu Dunn, Half The Sky, (Vintage Books, 2010), p. 154.

10 Hana Ali, More Than A Hero: Muhammad Ali's Life Lessons Through His Daughter's Eyes,1st Edition, (Atria: 1 May 2000).

11 Sara Bokker, "Why I Shed Bikini for Niqab: The New Symbol of Women's Liberation". I have downloaded this article from the internet website link: http://www.albalagh.net/women/0097.shtml

12 Nakata Khaula, "Veil: The View from the Inside". I have downloaded this article from the internet website link: http://www.albalagh.net/women/hijab.shtml

13 Nancy Gibbs, "Sexual Assaults on Female Soldiers: Don't Ask, Don't Tell", Time, 8 March 2010, p. 48.

14 John Leo, "When the Date Turns into Rape", Time. I have downloaded this article from the internet website link: http://www.time.com/time/magazine/article/0,9171,963854,00.html

15 This information is taken from the internet website: www.feminist.com.

16 Ibid

17 Ibid

18 Fiona Macrae, "Shocking figures show teenagers have a quarter of abortions in Britain", daily Mail (UK), 30 December 2011.

19 Dr. Mufti Abdul Wahid, Masail-i-Bihishti Zewar vol. 2, (Karachi: Majlis-i-Nasharyat-i-Islam, 2007), p. 38 - 42.

20 Committee of The Status of Woman in Islam, 1975.

21 Annie Besant, The Life and Teachings of Muhammad, (Madras: June 1932), p. 3.

22 Dr. Zakir Naik, "Most Common Questions asked by Non Muslims". I have downloaded this information from Dr. Naik's Islamic Research Foundation internet website link: http://www.irf.net/index.

php?option=com_content&view=article&id=404%3Apolygamy&catid
=71%3Amost-common-questions-asked-by-non-muslim&Itemid=199

23 J.E Clare McFarlane, The case for Polygamy, (London: 1934), p. 30.

24 Strasburger, V. C., University of New Mexico School of Medicine, Teen Pregnancy Rates in the USA, 2004. I have found this information at the internet website: http://www.aishtamid.org/pdfs/teen/TeenPregnancyRates.pdf

25 Dr. Mufti Abdul Wahid, Masail-i-Bihishti Zewar vol. 2, (Karachi: Majlis-i-Nasharyat-i-Islam, 2007), p. 353.

26 Ibid, p. 354.

27 Ibid, P. 353

28 This information is taken from the internet website link: http://www.women-health-info.com/266-Menstrual-period-side-effects.html

29 This information is taken from the internet website link: http://www.irf.net/index.php?option=com_content&view=article&id=391%3Ainheritance&catid=71%3Amost-common-questions-asked-by-non-muslim&Itemid=199

30 This quote is taken from the internet website: thinkexist.com.

31 Anton Nemilov, The Biological Tragedy of Women, (London: 1932), p. 76.

32 This organization is iERA ie Islamic Education and Research Academy.

Index

About The Author

Adeel Zeerak was born on 9th December 1968 in Karachi, the cosmopolitan city and the business hub of Pakistan. He received his early education at local Christian missionary schools at Karachi. He then joined D J Science College at Karachi for receiving his 'intermediate' college education. He graduated in Mechanical Engineering from NED University of Engineering and Technology, Karachi, Pakistan, in 1993. He did his Masters in Business Administration (MBA) with dual-specialization in Marketing and Finance from the Institute of Business Administration, Karachi, Pakistan, in 1999. Adeel Zeerak is also a 'Certified Supply Chain Professional' (CSCP) by APICS, Chicago, USA. In addition to that, he has attended numerous management and technical trainings including a four weeks training held at Malaysia on the topic of 'Workshop on Green-Productivity for trainers and consultants'. The training was sponsored by the Asian Productivity Organization, Tokyo, Japan.

While working as a management consultant at the Pakistan Institute of Management, Adeel Zeerak has himself developed and conducted various trainings throughout Pakistan mostly in the fields of General and Operations Management. He has also developed and delivered trainings for local and International organizations on the topics of Gender, and Feminism. He was involved in conducting trainings arranged for UNDP in collaboration with the Sindh Government for planning officers on the topic of 'Gender Sensitive Project Planning Skills'. These trainings were a part of a joint venture project between UNDP and the Government of Pakistan by the name of 'Gender Based Governance Systems (GBG).'

Adeel Zeerak has also served the manufacturing sector of Pakistan at various capacities for almost 13 years. During this period he was involved with the automotive sector.

Adeel Zeerak's study in Islam includes attending a 'Fahm-i-Deen' course by Idara Taleemat-i-Deenya, Jamia Madina Jadeed, Lahore, Pakistan. The course, with a proposed duration of one year, is developed by Dr. Mufti Abdul Wahid of Jamia Madina Jadeed, Lahore, Pakistan. Adeel Zeerak studied this course under the guidance of Maulana Abdus Sattar at Baitus Salam Masjid, Karachi, Pakistan. He has also attended a three months course on 'Basic themes of Islam' organized by Anjuman Khuddam-ul-Quran Sindh, Karachi, Pakistan. This organization was founded by Dr. Israr Ahmed (Late), a renowned Islamic scholar from Pakistan. Adeel Zeerak has also attended a one-month Islamic Course organized by Sirat-i-Mustaqim Foundation, Karachi, Pakistan. The course was designed and administered under the supervision of Dr. Ghulam Murtaza Malik (Late), who was also a renowned Islamic scholar from Pakistan.

In addition to the above mentioned formal trainings on Islam, Adeel Zeerak discovered a lot about Islam by reading books or listening to the lectures of various traditional Ulema including Mufti Rafi Usmani, Mufti Muhammad Taqi Usmani, Mufti Muhammad Shafi, Dr. Mufti Abdul Wahid, Maulana Syed Abul Hassan Ali Nadawi, Maulana Yousuf Ludhyanvi, Mufti Nazeer Ahmed, and Maulana Engineer Asad-ur-Rehman. Adeel Zeerak has also read many books or listened to the lectures of many other Islamic scholars like Maulana Abul Aala Maududi, Dr. Israr Ahmed, Dr. Ghulam Murtaza Malik, Professor Khursheed Ahmed, Dr. Zakir Naik, and Mr. Adnan Oktar (pen-name: Harun Yahya).

Adeel Zeerak is also a great admirer of Martial Arts. He is himself a Black Belt holder of the world renowned Japanese martial art of Shotokan Karate. He was also awarded an honorary Black Belt in world renowned Korean martial art of Tae Kwon Do for his contributions and services for the art.

Adeel Zeerak's career as an author started with the successful launching of his first book 'Islam: A Superior System of Life' on September 11, 2012. He maintains a personal library with a collection on various topics including Engineering, Medical and General Sciences, Management, Economics, Finance, Martial Arts, Mathematics, History, and Islam. You can contact Adeel Zeerak at adeelzeerak@hotmail.com